The Wonders of Heaven

by Rev. Donald F. Ginkel

A study of heaven from the Holy Bible

Ten thousand times ten thousand, in sparkling raiment bright,
The armies of the ransomed saints throng up the steeps of light,
'Tis finished, all is finished, their fight with death and sin,
Fling open wide the golden gates, and let the victors in.

Bring near Thy great salvation, Thou Lamb for sinners slain;
Fill up the roll of Thine elect, then take Thy power and reign,
Appear, desire of nations, Thine exiles long for home;
Show in the heavens Thy promised sign; Thou Prince
     and Savior, come! AMEN!

Henry Alford

Additional copies of this book and other Bible studies for young people and adults plus other materials for church growth may be ordered from Church Press, Inc. Ask for a brochure.

CHURCH PRESS, INC.
Rev. Donald F. Ginkel
Toll Free: 1-888-772-8878
www.churchpress.com

Contents

The Many Wonders of Heaven

The Many Wonders of Heaven
Copyrighted © 1993 by Donald F. Ginkel
Revised edition copyrighted, 2000
All rights reserved

Library of Congress Catalog Card Number: TX 3-575-145

ISBN 0-9642122-0-X

Printed in the United States of America

Lesson 1

THE MANY WONDERS OF HEAVEN

The Wonder of Entrance

Death, it is said, is the terminal conclusion of life on earth. Death reduces man's body to a few minerals and chemical compounds. Death strikes with a numbing and terrifying force. Death comes on its own terms, not ours, and in its own bitter time, not ours. Death is the end, they say.

George Bernard Shaw wrote, "The statistics on death are quite impressive. One out of one people die." We humans have a strikingly high mortality rate. One bumper sticker put it this way: "Eat right, exercise well — die anyway."

Some people, like those in Christian Science, say that death is an illusion; it is an incorrect state of mind. Folks who deny death deceive themselves. Society today has great difficultly facing the matter of death. Billy Graham once called death the twentieth century pornography. It is to this age what sex was to the Victorians. Most people would rather not talk about it.

But the Bible talks about death. It says, "The sons of men... are but *grass*" (Isaiah 51:12). Again, "There is... a time to be born and a time to *die*" (Ecclesiastes 3:2). You know the saying, "The only sure things are death and taxes." Some people can figure out ways of beating the tax laws, but none has figured out how to beat death.

If death must come — and it must — we want it to be quick, quiet, and painless. And then what? Is it really the end?

The wonder of all wonders is that, because of Jesus, death becomes for us the very doorway to everlasting life in heaven. The joy of our eternal home must be preceded by death. Through it we go Home (Psalm 23)!

Opening Hymn

Abide with me, fast falls the eventide. The darkness deepens;
Lord with me abide. When other helpers fail and comforts flee,
Help of the helpless, oh, abide with me.

Swift to its close ebbs out life's little day; Earth's joys grow dim,
Its glories pass away; Change and decay in all around I see;
O Thou who changest not, abide with me.

Opening Prayer

Our gracious and loving God, we thank You and magnify You for making us members of Your blessed family, the one true Church built upon Your Son, Jesus Christ. Our thinking concerning death needs some assistance. We confess that we still tend to view death as the final end. Help us move toward Your view of our impending departure from this world. Give us grace to see death, not as the end, but as the beginning of a new life with You in heaven. We thank You, dear Jesus, for saving us, body and soul, by Your holy suffering and death upon the cross. Grant that each of us in this Bible study may be touched by Your Word. We await Your guidance. In Your name. Amen.

Heaven Impossible Because of Sin

1. Adam and Eve were created by God for a happy life in the Garden of Eden. Read Genesis 2:15-17 and briefly summarize: _____

    _____

    _____

    _____

    Read and summarize Genesis 3:6-8,23:

    _____

    _____

    _____

    _____

    _____

2. We have tried to soften the blow of death. We have renamed the Undertaker. We now call him the _____

    The coffin. We now call it a _____

    People who have died we now say _____

    Many people have never been to a funeral. It seems too grotesque for them. What accounts for all this denial? _____

    _____

    _____

    Death has been substantially removed from the home. My grandmother and my little sister died at home for everyone to see. That was at Nicollet, MN. Not many people die at home these days. That's what hospitals and convalescent homes are for. What advantages are there for dying at home? _____

    _____

3. St. Paul writes: "Just as sin entered the world through one man,

and death through sin, and in this way *death* came to *all men,* because *all sinned*" (Romans 5:12). Note the universality of sin and death. Note both our original sin and actual sin. And note the result of sin: spiritual, physical, and eternal death. Isaiah writes: "Your iniquities have separated you from your God" (Isaiah 59:2). What can we rightfully conclude on the basis of these verses?_____

On the other hand, what does man, by nature, think? _____

_____

4. A national magazine conducted a public opinion poll asking, "What are your chances of getting into heaven?" One man in Michigan said: "50–50. As I grow older I think my chances are improving" (Do senior citizens get a special break?). A man in his late twenties said, "I'd say my chances are about eight-five percent. I don't think the exam will be that tough." Yet, St. John, inspired by the Spirit, says of the New Jerusalem: "*Nothing impure* will ever enter it, nor will anyone who does what is shameful or deceitful" (Revelation 21:27). How many sins would it take to keep a person out of heaven? _____

Heaven Possible Because of Jesus

1. Death looks like a real champion when a person stops breathing. But Christ has conquered death by taking our sins to the cross and there dying for them in our place. Hebrews 2:14-15 says, "He

too shared in their humanity so that by His death He might destroy him who holds the power of death – that is, the devil – and *free those* who all their lives were *held in slavery* by their *fear of death.*" And 2 Timothy 1:10, "Christ Jesus, who has *destroyed death* and has *brought life* and *immortality* to light through the gospel." What effect should the italicized words have on us? _____

_____

_____

2   We Christians should have a genuine ambivalence towards death. It is an enemy of our flesh. But Christ has won such an astounding victory over the power of death that it has been reduced to a non-threat. See what St. Paul says: "The sting of death is sin, and the power of sin is the law. But thanks be to God! He gives us the victory *through our Lord Jesus Christ*" (1 Corinthians 15:56-57).

Journey to Heaven Begins at Conversion

The journey to Heaven begins the moment a person has saving faith in Jesus. Divide your class into six groups. Each group study one of the verses below and then share with the class (Pay close attention to the tense of the verbs).

John 5:24 _____

John 6:47 _____

Titus 3:5 _____

Galatians 3:26 _____

John 17:3 _____

John 20:31 _____

True or False: Every believer in this Bible study is a member of God's Kingdom this very moment and is united with all other believers on earth and in heaven. Prove your answer.

Entrance Into Heaven Occurs at Death

We seem to be like the woman who was trying to squeeze affection from a neighbor's attractive child. She knelt down by the girl and said, "Do you love me, darling?" A little nod. "Then put your arms around me and give me a big kiss!" The child complied and then continued playing. The woman's encircling arms held their prisoner. "How much to you love me, precious?" she insisted. "Would you cry if I died?" The little girl nodded. "Show me how you would cry," the woman urged. "Die first!" the child suggested. Many of us want to experience the joys of heaven without the experience of death.

1.   What are we really afraid of? What is death? Romanticists call it "man's last great venture." Poets speak of it as "crossing the river" or "putting out to sea." The Bible teaches, however, that physical

death is the separation of the soul from the body. It is not the end of existence, but a departure. In the following passages name the people and their destinations.

Genesis 25:8 _____

Philippians 1:23 _____

Luke 16:22-23 _____

Luke 23:43 _____

When Scripture speaks of the dead as resting or sleeping, it is referring to the body. "They will *rest* from their labor" (Revelation 14:13). "There the weary are at *rest*" (Job 3:17). "I will *sleep* in death" says David (Psalm 13:3).

2. Near-death experiences are interesting, but they are inconsequential. Are these experiences equal or superior to

    Scriptural teaching? _____

    Unbelievers report the same experiences as believers. Their focus is a great white light and warm feelings — hardly close to the reports given in the Holy Record by Paul and John. What dangers do you see when people give near-death experiences too much

    attention? _____

    _____

    _____

3. Definition of Biblical terms:

    a. **Heaven** — the vast expanse of the sky and beyond. Also, the dwelling place of God and the redeemed. The Bible refers to heaven approximately 550 times. Name some conclusions we

        should come to in view of this high number: _____

        _____

        _____

    b. **Paradise** — of Persian origin denoting a garden or a park. Also, the home of God's children.

    c. **Sheol** — one meaning is the grave (Job 17:16; Isaiah 38:10).

Also, the realm of the dead, much like our "hereafter" or "beyond" or "to die and depart from the land of the living" (Genesis 37:35; Job 7:9). In some passages it is the place of the impenitent sinner (Numbers 16:30; Proverbs 5:5).

d. **Hades** — a non-Biblical Greek word used to translate the Hebrew Sheol. It may mean "the grave" (Revelation 2:13-14) or "death" (Acts 2:27,31). It is also used to denote the place of torment for unbelievers (Matthew 11:23; Luke 16:23).

e. **Gehenna** — originally the name of the deep ravine southwest of Jerusalem where children were offered as sacrifices (2 Kings 23:10). The Jews turned it into a burning garbage dump.

f. **Abyssos** — meaning bottomless and unbounded and denotes the deep (Genesis 1:2), great anguish of soul (Psalm 71:20), the place of the dead, the grave (Romans 10:7), and hell, the place of evil spirits ruled by Satan (Revelation 9:1,11;17:8).

4. Is there a waiting period at death, a place like purgatory? Many modern-day Catholics no longer subscribe to this belief. What is purgatory? Purgatory is the teaching that a member of the church, no matter how devout, must suffer temporal punishment for his sin. Jesus, however, became our "purgatory," and He took our hell. "When He had brought about the *purgation* of sins, He  took His seat at the right hand of Majesty on high" (Hebrews 1:3) according to the NEB translation. The tense of the Greek verb "purge" is aorist; it means that it was one action and is unrepeatable! What does the belief of purgatory do to:

a. The Gospel? _____

_____

_____

b. The person facing death? _____

_____

_____

5.   Eschatology is a theological term and concerns itself with a study of the last things, including death. What do we learn about death from these verses?

    a.   Ecclesiastes 12:7 _____

    _____

    b.   2 Samuel 14:14a _____

    _____

    c.   2 Corinthians 5:1 What is the contrast in buildings and what does it teach us? _____

    _____

    What is the encouragement? _____

    _____

    Read 5:4. What is being conveyed with the word "tent"?

    _____

    One Christian said, "I am not longing to die, but I am longing for what death brings." What is meant by that statement?

    _____

    Is there any way to get to heaven without passing through death (think carefully)? _____

    _____

    Read 5:7-8. What is Paul teaching us here? _____

    _____

6.   R. C. Lenski (2 Cor., p. 1011) writes: "The things not seen shall presently turn to the things seen. This must come, otherwise faith would trust in something that does not exist; it would be like the faith of the worldling who trusts in something that does not exist and that he will, therefore, never see. He is like the man who *thinks* that he has a million dollars in the bank, who goes on in this fatuous faith, and who, when he at last tries to draw out his million, finds that he never had a million, finds that he owes a million and cannot pay. We trust that our bank has a million

dollars that was deposited for us by Christ; He has, indeed, deposited them for us, and when at death we come to draw them out, they will be handed out to us, we shall get sight of every penny of them, shall have them in our hands forever."

Comment on Lenski's statement.

7. Read Luke 16:22. For centuries these words have made an indelible impression upon believers everywhere. The beggar was not just escorted, but actually carried by angels to Abraham's bosom (a Jewish designation for heaven). What an experience that must have been for Lazarus. We have every reason to believe these words. This is the only parable Jesus told where He put a name on a person. Many Christians believe this story was played out in real life. Lazarus' body had been covered with sores. He lay begging at the gate of the rich man until his death. Suddenly he found himself carried by the mighty angels to heaven! We should believe that holy angels will attend our deathbeds and will carry our souls safely to heaven.

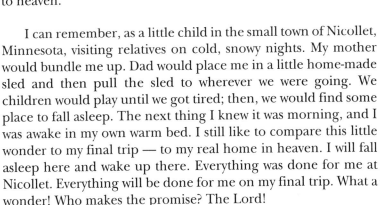

I can remember, as a little child in the small town of Nicollet, Minnesota, visiting relatives on cold, snowy nights. My mother would bundle me up. Dad would place me in a little home-made sled and then pull the sled to wherever we were going. We children would play until we got tired; then, we would find some place to fall asleep. The next thing I knew it was morning, and I was awake in my own warm bed. I still like to compare this little wonder to my final trip — to my real home in heaven. I will fall asleep here and wake up there. Everything was done for me at Nicollet. Everything will be done for me on my final trip. What a wonder! Who makes the promise? The Lord!

Read Psalm 91:11-12. What are you specifically promised here? _____

> There let my way appear Steps unto heav'n;
> All that Thou sendest me In mercy giv'n;
> Angels to beckon me Nearer, my God, to Thee,
> Nearer, my God to Thee, Nearer to Thee.
> — Sarah F. Roams

Astronauts sometimes must fear tragedy in space, but we Christians can be confident. Are you? _____

Why? _____

_____

In 1686 Amilie Juliane wrote this comforting verse —

> Then may death come today, tomorrow,
> I know in Christ I perish not;
> He grants the peace that stills all sorrow,
> Gives me a robe without a spot.
> My God, for Jesus' sake I pray
> Thy peace may bless my dying day.

8. One little girl said: "Only good people go to heaven. The other people go to Florida where it's hot all the time!" She is totally wrong on the first point and on most of the second one. While death is the "doorway" to heaven for the believer, it is the "doorway" to hell for unbelievers. Jesus said, "The rich man also *died* and was buried. In *hell*, where he was in torment..." (Luke 16:23). Why do you suppose that so many people do not want to listen to or discuss this terrible tragedy? _____

_____

_____

Journey to Heaven Complete at the Resurrection

Actress Drew Barrymore is really into her cat, and she literally wants it to be that way, too. A newspaper article quotes her as saying, "My cat is such an important part of my life that if I die before him I want a little bit of my ashes put in his food so that I can live inside him." In contrast we Christians have a wish or, better yet, a strong statement to make. In the Apostles' Creed we confess: "I believe in the resurrection of the body." The last four words in Greek are *sarkos anastas* and in Latin *carnis rectionem,* which literally translated are "resurrection of the flesh." But how is this possible?

1. Jesus said, "I tell you the truth, unless a kernel of wheat falls to the ground and dies, it remains only a single seed. But *if it dies,* it produces many seeds" (John 12:24). On the basis of this verse St. Augustine wrote, "The death of Christ was the death of the most fertile grain of wheat."

    True or False: There can be no following fruit (that's us on the Day of Resurrection) without Christ's death. Just as His body died and rose again, so shall we. Prove your answer with specific words from verse 24:

    _____

2. Our journey to heaven will not be complete until our renewed body and soul are reunited on the great Day of Resurrection. What is stressed in these verses?

    John 5:28-29 _____

    _____

    1 Thessalonians 4:13-14 _____

    _____

    1 Corinthians 15:51-52 _____

    _____

    Until the resurrection our souls will be "at home with the Lord" (2 Corinthians 5:8). On the last day the trumpets will sound and the Lord will appear triumphant and glorious in the sky with all the holy angels. He will raise our bodies from the earth, new and beautiful just like His body. The journey will be finished!

3. Read Matthew 25:31-34,41,46. This judgment is not to determine where we will spend eternity; that was already settled the moment

we became believers and was reaffirmed at the moment of death. This is a review of the works we produced, either good works flowing out of saving faith or evil works flowing out of unbelief. All unbelievers will go away to eternal punishment, and we Christians will go Home with the Lord.

Concluding Thoughts

1. We need to be reminded again and again of the hopelessness of life without Jesus and the hope of heaven. Comedian Woody Allen was asked by an interviewer, "Aren't you glad that you will achieve immortality through achievements?" Allen gloomily responded, "Who cares about achieving immortality through achievements? I am interested in achieving immortality through not dying." What does his statement tell us not only about Woody

   Allen, but all men by nature? _____

   _____

2. Paul McCartney, the former Beatle, was asked if he believed in life after death. He replied, "When we were kids, we always used to say, 'OK, whoever dies first, get a message through...' When John (Lennon) died, I thought, 'Well, maybe we'll get a message,' because I know he knew the deal. I haven't heard a

   message from John." What does his statement tell us? _____

   _____

3. True or False: Death is a natural part of life. Defend your answer.

4. My son, Mark, here in Denver, CO, has advanced Melanoma and has been fighting it for four years. Three years ago a clergy friend of mine had a daughter in college who had cancer and after two years she died. He suffered much over this. After the funeral some of the pastors in the area tried to encourage him with words like, "You should be happy. Now she is in heaven." Comment on

   their "encouragement": _____

5. Try to imagine for a moment that you are not a Christian. How

   does the thought strike you? _____

If you were an unbeliever, what would you want any of your Christian friends to say or do or not say or do? _____

_____

6. Has your desire to get to heaven become weaker or stronger in the last year? _____ In either case share why it did: _____

_____

7. Read Ecclesiastes 9:5-6. What is your reaction? Why? _____

_____

_____

_____

8. Recently two obituaries appeared side by side in a local paper. Following their date of death is the most significant sentence I could find for each.

Rita Ann Ramel, 25, Overland Park, KS, died Thursday, July 31 from surgery complications. **She is rejoicing in the presence of her Lord and Savior Jesus Christ.**

Allen David Smith (not real name), 20, Olathe, KS, passed away Friday, August 1, as a result of an automobile accident. **For Allen: Not flesh of my flesh, nor bone of my bone, but still miraculously my own. Never forget for a single minute you didn't grow under my heart but in it. You know how much we love you, Allen.**

Discuss what each significant sentence seems to be saying.

9. David says, "Even though I walk through the valley of the shadow of death, I will *fear no evil*, for You are with me; Your rod and your staff, they *comfort* me" (Psalm 23:4). What makes you fearful of this walk? What makes you confident? Let this be a time of sharing. _____

_____

Closing Hymn

I fear no foe with Thee at hand to bless;
Ills have no weight, and tears no bitterness.
Where is death's sting? Where, grave, thy victory?
I triumph still if Thou abide with me.

Hold Thou Thy cross before my closing eyes,
Shine through the gloom, and point me to the skies;
Heav'n's morning breaks, and earth's vain shadows flee;
In life, in death, O Lord, abide with me.

Closing Prayer

Lesson 2

THE MANY WONDERS OF HEAVEN

The Wonder of God

The seven wonders of the ancient world are: 1. The pyramids of Egypt. 2. The Pharos of Alexandria. 3. The walls and hanging gardens of Babylon. 4. The temple of Diana at Ephesus. 5. The statue of the Olympian Zeus by Phidias. 6. The mausoleum erected by Queen Artemisia at Halicarnassus. 7. The Colossus of Rhodes.

But how would all these wonders of the world today — how would all of them put together compare to the wonder of the full glory of God in heaven? Supercolossal, doubled-up adjectives used to describe earthly beauty will be totally lacking when we see God.

A Sunday School teacher asked her class to draw a picture from the Bible, any picture they wanted. When she asked one boy what he was drawing he said, "God." So she explained, "But no one has seen Him. We don't know what God looks like." To which the boy replied, "We will when I get done." Well, here on earth it cannot be done, but just wait. Soon we going to see God in all His resplendent glory. Oh, what a day! Oh, what a wonder it will be!

Opening Hymn

Holy, holy, holy, Lord God Almighty!
Early in the morning our song shall rise to Thee.
Holy, holy, holy, merciful and mighty!
God in three Persons, blessed Trinity.

Holy, holy, holy! All the saints adore Thee,
Casting down their golden crowns around the glassy sea.
Cherubim and seraphim falling down before Thee,
Which wert and art and evermore shalt be.

Opening Prayer

Dear Father, Son, and Holy Spirit, angels always glorify You. The saints in heaven see you and praise You. How can we, weak and sinful as we are, have their joy and worthily present our praise to You? O Father, You have given us life and preserved us. O precious Savior, You have given Yourself as our ransom from eternal ruin. O sanctifying Spirit, You have called us to a living faith in the Savior. Our ever-glorious God, speed the day when we join You in Your house. Please pour down showers of blessings upon us at home, at work and play, in church, and in this Bible study. We want to know more about what it will be like to see You, not just by faith, but face to face. We ask this in the saving name of Jesus. Amen.

Soon and Very Soon

A little boy was riding alone on a train on a hot day many years ago when there was no air conditioning. It was uncomfortable. The desert of Arizona was not pretty. A lady sitting beside the boy asked him, "Are you tired of the long trip?" The boy smiled and said, "I'm a little tired, but I don't mind it much. You see, I'm going to see my father in Los Angeles. He'll be there waiting for me."

Sometimes we get a little tired of our travel through life, but it is great to know that we are going to see our Father soon because of Jesus. He'll be there at the end of life's journey. We'll meet Him. We'll see Him. That's first when we arrive! Right now we confess with (what is the accompanying condition in each case?):

- **DAVID** — "And I – in righteousness I will *see Your face*; when I awake, I will be satisfied with *seeing Your likeness*" (Psalm 17:15).

- **JOB**— "And after my skin has been destroyed, yet in my flesh *I will see God*; I myself will *see Him with my own eyes* – I, and not another. How my heart yearns within me" (Job 19:26-27).

- **JESUS** — "Blessed are the pure in heart, for they will *see God*" (Matthew 5:8).

- **PAUL** — "Now we see but a poor reflection as in a mirror; then we shall *see face to face*. Now I know in part; then I shall know fully, even as I am fully known" (1 Corinthians 13:12).

- **JOHN** — "We know that when He appears, we shall be like Him, for we shall *see Him* as He is" (1 John 3:2).

- **JOHN** again — "They will *see His face*, and His name will be on their foreheads" (Revelation 22:4).

Face to face I shall behold Him, Far beyond the starry sky;
Face to face, in all His glory, I shall see Him by and by.
Carrie E. Beck

And what will we see? It will be something very different from what we "see" by faith here on earth.

His Glory

1. Have you ever looked at the sun? What did you see? Why? _____

    _____

2. What do the following verses tell us?

    a.   1 Timothy 6:15b-16 _____

    _____

    b. John 17:24 _____

c.   1 Peter 4:13 _____

d.   Revelation 21:11 _____

e.   Revelation 21:23 _____

3.   Read Matthew 17:1-2. What did the three disciples really see?

_____

_____

How bright was the light? _____

True or False: Jesus will not shine any brighter in heaven than He did on the Mount of Transfiguration (Revelation 21:23).

Prove your answer: _____

_____

4.   Read Isaiah 60:19-20. What are some of the limitations of the sun

and moon here on earth? _____

_____ What is the light source in heaven? _____

How is it described and what does it suggest? _____

_____

5.   Read Ezekiel 1:4-28. The prophet has trouble finding appropriate nouns and adjectives to describe the scene, and the scene is real. The wheels that moved in concert, the sparkling jewels, the lightning, and the brilliant light are pictures of God's power and glory. Pay close attention to verses 4 and 16-28. We cannot fully understand this description of

God's glory, but Ezekiel is endeavoring to paint a picture of the sovereignty, majesty, and glory of God. But the picture is beyond our understanding. Even in the vision the prophet cannot come face to face. Speaking to Moses God said, "You *cannot see my face*, for no one (in a sinful, mortal body) may see Me and live" (Exodus 33:20).

a. What immediate effect did the vision have upon Ezekiel?

_____

b. What effect do you suppose your actually seeing God in heavenly glory will have upon you? _____

_____

c. True or False: Ezekiel saw God's glory, but only through filtered lenses, if you will, but the saints in heaven see God in His full glory.

d. Which words in verses 26 - 28 show the difficulty Ezekiel had in describing what he saw? _____

_____

e. Why do you think God gave Ezekiel this vision? _____

_____

f. Why was it written down? _____

_____

6. How did a limited revelation of God's glory appear according to Exodus 24:15-17? _____

Read Exodus 33:18-23. What was Moses' request? _____

What was God's response? _____

_____

What does this reveal about God? _____

_____

7. Read Revelation 1:12-16. John had seen the Lord on the Mount of Transfiguration many years before, but now he sees Him more

fully revealed. The imagery is that of high and royal majesty. What effect did the sight of the Lord's glory have on John (verse 17)?

_____

What effect do you think this sight has upon all the saints in heaven right now? _____

7.   The wonder of all wonders is that soon we, too, shall see the Lord revealed in all His glory. Don't let a day go by without thinking about this. It can turn a sad day into a glad day.

Glory be to God the Father, Glory be to God the Son,
Glory be to God the Spirit: Great Jehovah, Three in One!
Glory, glory While eternal ages run!
Horatious Bonar

His Holiness

"And they were calling to one another: '*Holy, holy, holy* is the LORD Almighty'" (Isaiah 6:3). This was the antiphonal singing of the seraphim that Isaiah saw and heard as he looked at God on His

Throne in heaven. Holy means sinless, pure, perfect, to hit the mark or bull's eye. It describes the absolute ethical purity of God. They looked at God and sang holy, holy, holy — you and I will do the same thing when we look upon Him.

"He who called you is *holy*... for it is written: 'Be holy, because *I am holy*'" (1 Peter 1:15-16). God is holy in and of Himself. He has freedom from evil on the one hand and, on the other, absolute moral perfection. To see His holiness will be to see His goodness, both of which are revealed in Jesus Christ now and forever. This will be our joy, and what a joy it will be!

How will God's holiness appear to us according to Exodus 15:11?

_____

Read Revelation 4:8. The four living creatures appear to be seraphim who have six wings (Isaiah 6:2-3). What is their response to seeing God? _____

R. C. Lenski writes: "Holiness is the attribute which separates God infinitely from all that is sin and sinful in a way such as no pagan ever conceived... it is a holiness revealed and active from above to those beneath so as to make them holy by salvation or to cast them away forever in judgment" (*St. John's Revelation*, p. 186).

True or False: In view of the above statements our first words, upon seeing God in heaven, might well be, "Holy, holy, holy!"

His Love

With a new "20/20" vision in heaven we will see and experience God's love which is associated with His holiness. "God is *love*" (1 John 4:8). The Greek word for love is αγαπε (agape). It is an unconditional love, whereas ours is frequently conditional.

It is directed toward personal beings — sinful beings. It revealed itself to Adam and Eve in the promise of the Messiah (Genesis 3:15). It expressed itself over and over again in the Old Testament. The great prophet wrote: "In His *love* and *mercy* He redeemed them (God's people)" (Isaiah 63:9). In the New Testament God's love is Christo-centric and cross-centered (John 3:16). The cross of Calvary with Jesus hanging on it for sinners is the final definition of "agape." It is the focal point and fullest expression of God's love. That is what we will see soon.

Read 1 John 4:7-10 and record those words which speak of God's love: _____

_____

What is the two-fold result of God's love in Revelation 1:5b,6?

_____

_____

F. M. Lehman wrote and we confess —

The love of God is greater far Than tongue or pen can ever tell;
It goes beyond the highest star, And reaches to the lowest hell;
The guilty pair, bowed down with care, God gave His Son to win;
  His erring child He reconciled, And pardoned from his sin.
O love of God, how rich and pure! How measureless and strong!
  It shall for evermore endure The saints' and angels' song.

Lovers find great joy in looking into the face of their beloved, but their joy is fleeting. Our joy in the presence of God's love will abide forever. We look forward to this. We agree with David: "One thing I ask of the LORD, this is what I seek: that I may dwell in the house of the LORD all the days of my life, to *gaze upon the beauty* of the LORD" (Psalm 27:4).

His Throne

Jesus said, "He who swears by heaven swears by *God's throne* and by the One who sits on it" (Matthew 23:22).

1. How is this scene described in Ezekiel 1:26? _____

_____

2. Read Isaiah 6:1-4. This was not a dream. Isaiah says, "I *saw* the Lord seated on a *throne.*" In the New Testament John comments on this scene in John 12:41. Isaiah saw the Lord seated on a

    throne which was _____ and _____.

    This description is anthropomorphic which means that Isaiah saw the Lord in human form. This is a condescension of the invisible God so that the prophet could see and comprehend. He who is called Lord (*Adonai* or Supreme Ruler) in verse 1 is called *Yahweh* (His covenant or redemptive name) in verse 3. What effect did

    this vision have on Isaiah? _____

_____

    Will this sight have the same effect on us when we get to heaven?

    Prove your answer: _____

_____

3. While the class reads Revelation 4:2-6 have someone count the
    number of times the word "throne" appears in Revelation 4 (This
    is the great throne chapter of the Bible) and write it here: _____
    There is no greater symbol of power, rule, and dominion in
    heaven than the throne which is why it caught John's attention
    immediately. Revelation 5:7 indicates God is sitting on the throne
    in contrast to other verses which speak of the Lamb on His
    throne. The beauty and glory of God are reflected in the
    surroundings. Why do you think that you will be attracted to the

    throne when you get to heaven? _____

    _____

His Dwelling Place

Heaven is where God dwells with the angels and with His children.
"From heaven the LORD looks down and sees all mankind; from His
dwelling place He watches all who live on earth" (Psalm 33:13-14).
"There is a river whose streams make glad the city of God, the holy
place where the Most High *dwells*" (Psalm 46:4). "For this is what the
high and lofty One says – He who lives forever, whose name is holy:
'I *live* in a high and *holy place*'" (Isaiah 57:15). "In My Father's *house*
(οικια — a dwelling place, a home) are many rooms; if it were not so,
I would have told you. I am going there to prepare a place for you"
(John 14:2).

True or False: Heaven cannot contain God, yet it is His dwelling
place.

His Temple

Two major buildings were present in many
ancient cities, the palace and the temple. In
heaven God's rule is signified by the throne,
and there is a temple which indicates He
will be worshiped. The tabernacle made for
easy movement, and the temple in
Jerusalem had been the focal point of God's
presence with His people on earth.

Jesus says, "Him who overcomes I will make a pillar in the
temple of My God. Never again will he leave it" (Revelation 3:12). Like

a pillar in a building, the Christian always remains in the presence of God in heaven at all times. "They (the redeemed) are before the throne of God and serve Him day and night in His *temple*, and He who sits on the throne will spread His tent over them" (Revelation 7:15).

But in Revelation 21:22 John says, "I did not see a *temple* in the city, because the Lord God Almighty and the Lamb are its *temple*." The temple in heaven is not a place where God dwells because God Himself is the temple! Heaven is completely filled with God's glorious presence so that everyone will at all times be with Him and He with them.

Concluding Thoughts

When one becomes a Christian, the reality of heaven becomes an accepted fact. In this Lesson we learned that the greatest wonder in all of heaven is the wonder of God.

When Isaiah saw the scenes described in this Lesson, we read these words: "'Woe to me!' I cried. 'I am ruined! For I am a man of unclean lips, and I live among a people of unclean lips, and my eyes have seen the King, the LORD Almighty'" (Isaiah 6:5).Oh, what an infinite majesty is God's majesty. Oh, what a glory. Oh, what a throne. Oh, what a sight! Soon we will join the redeemed, too.

True or False: If a believer looks forward to seeing any of his loved ones in heaven before seeing God, chances are that he is not a Christian. Could this really happen? Why? _____

* What are some thoughts about God in heaven that simply amaze you now? _____

_____

_____

Closing Hymn

Holy, holy, holy! Though the darkness hide Thee,
Though the eye made blind by sin Thy glory may not see,
Only Thou art holy; there is none beside Thee,

Perfect in pow'r, in love and purity.

Holy, holy, holy! Lord God Almighty!
All Thy works shall praise Thy name in earth and sky and sea.
Holy, holy, holy, merciful and mighty!
God in three Persons, blessed Trinity!

Closing Prayer

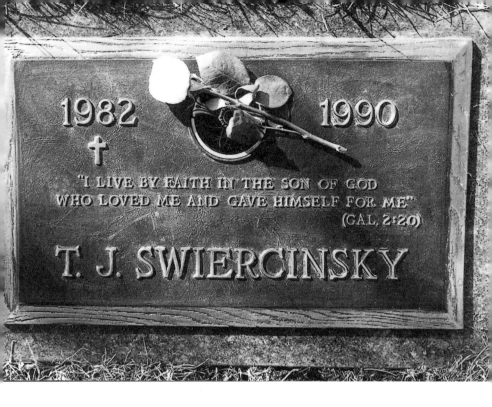

Lesson 3

THE MANY WONDERS OF HEAVEN

The Wonder of
the Saints

This is T. J.'s grave marker. He was a very pretty boy in so many ways. He loved people, to have fun, to learn, to be a friend to the friendless. He especially loved Jesus. He took piano lessons so that he could play at worship (and he did). He never missed church, ever. Why? Because he really loved Jesus. He read his Bible to his mother every evening. His favorite book was the Bible, and he said, "When I grow up I'd like to be a pastor." He did and said all these things with great joy and a sparkle in his eye.

At 3:15 one afternoon he was run over and killed by his own

school bus! Only seven years old. It was the most moving and awesome funeral service I have ever conducted. Now T. J. is in heaven and so are all our loved ones who died believing in Jesus as their Savior. And they are doing just fine! That's the portrait this Lesson will paint, and what a picture it is. Let's sing one of T. J.'s favorite hymns (If you don't know the tune, just read the words aloud).

Opening Hymn

I am Jesus' little lamb, Ever glad at heart I am;
For my Shepherd gently guides me,
Knows my need and well provides me,
Loves me ev'ry day the same, Even calls me by my name.

Day by day, at home, away, Jesus is my staff and stay.
When I hunger, Jesus feeds me,
Into pleasant pastures leads me;
When I thirst, He bids me go Where the quiet waters flow.

Who so happy as I am, Even now the Shepherd's lamb?
And when my short life is ended,
By His angel host attended,
He shall fold me to His breast, There within His arms to rest.

Opening Prayer

Dear Jesus, we give You all praise and glory for providing for our salvation by your suffering and death. O Holy Spirit, we praise You for bringing us to saving faith in our dear Savior. Dear God, we pour out our hearts in praise for all the saints we have known, including dear friends and some who were even related to us by blood, who are now with You in heaven. Thank You, God! Praise be to You! We miss them very much. Give us grace in this hour that we may have comfort, hope, and happiness. Please help us take a little peek at the saints in glory, and help us look forward to the great changes we will experience the moment we join You. In Jesus' name. Amen.

I'd Rather Be . . .

You finish the sentence. I'll give you a choice — choose one. If I honestly had to choose one of the following right now it would be:
( ) one week in Maui, ( ) one week in Stanley, KS, ( ) forever in

heaven, or ( ) 150 years right where I live now. I know that my Bible class teacher and Pastor Ginkel want me to check heaven, but, honestly, I would take _____

_____

Assuming you wrote "heaven," get ready for a pop quiz. One Saturday afternoon was of my members, John, called and asked that I come to his home right away. When I arrived I found the children in the yard crying. John was in the bathroom attempting to resuscitate his wife (37 years old) who had suffered severe heatstroke. I helped John, but our efforts were futile. We picked her body up, placed it on her bed, and called the funeral home. Before we asked the four children to come in John and I knelt at the foot of the bed in prayer. When we finished I said, "John, honestly now, between you and me and God, what do you think?" He looked at me. Tears were running down both of his cheeks. He said, "Pastor, I'm so happy for Phoebe. I'm so happy for her." I said, "Why?" "Well," he said with a quivering voice, "I and the children are going to miss her very much, but now she is with the Lord she loved so much, and she is happier by far with the Lord than she would be with us." You should know that the next morning, Sunday morning, at the first service, John and the children were in church in the front pew. I missed her, too. She was very active in our evangelism outreach program and in teaching God's Word to children. Now I realize the question is hypothetical, but, what would you have said if you were John? _____

_____

Many people are not anxious to go to heaven right now. "Lord, I haven't been to Hawaii yet!" "We haven't built our dream home yet!" How sad that some folks want to hang on to things here which will perish and the love of which can lead to eternal ruin. Some people would prefer to stay here indefinitely rather than go to heaven.

1. Why do you suppose some people would rather stay right where they are than go to heaven? _____

    Have you ever felt this way? _____ Why? _____

2. True or False: On a scale of 1 to 10, our new life in heaven is at least a 10 in comparison to the lifestyles of the rich and famous.

3. What does St. Paul remind us of in:

   2 Corinthians 5:4a? _____

   2 Corinthians 4:18? _____

   2 Corinthians 5:1? _____

This lesson will focus on the status and condition of the saints in heaven and following lessons on the activity.

Names Written

Harriet E. Buell said it so well:

> I once was an outcast stranger on earth,
> A sinner by choice, and an alien by birth;
> But I've been adopted, my name's written down,
> An heir to a mansion, a robe, and a crown.

Jesus said to the disciples who were casting out demons, "Do not rejoice that the spirits submit to you, but that your *names are written in heaven*" (Luke 10:20). We are to rejoice in something very personal and which was not done *by* us but *for* us. God has enrolled us in the book of life, and even Satan cannot erase it.

1. What is your name (write it out)? _____

2. True or False: Right now this name is recorded in the book of life in heaven. √ 20

3. What benefit might come your way if you consciously and daily thought about Luke 10:20b? Lois Filipiak

   _____

4. What truths does Jesus add in:

   Revelation 3:5? _____

   _____

Revelation 21:27b? _____

_____

Citizenship

"But our *citizenship* is in heaven" (Philippians 3:20). The Greek word for "citizenship" is πολιτευμα and would be better translated "commonwealth." A commonwealth is made up of a body of people constituting a state or community in which the citizens have certain rights and privileges. Commonwealths on earth usually grant temporary permits to foreigners; no such arrangements, however, exist in heaven.

Paul reminds Gentile converts, "*Remember* that at that time you were *separate* from Christ, *excluded* from *citizenship* in Israel and *foreigners* to the covenants of the promise, without hope and without God in the world" (Ephesians 2:12).

1. What does the very first word tell you to do all the time (think the entire verse through carefully)? _____

_____

2. What is the benefit of doing this? _____

_____

3. True or False: A person is either a citizen of heaven or else he may not get in.

4. True or False: I am a citizen in good standing in the kingdom of heaven and if I died right now I would immediately claim my citizenship in heaven for sure!

Bride of Christ

Have you ever seen an ugly bride? All brides are beautiful. The bride of Christ is the *Una Sancta* and is perfect beauty to the Bridegroom, the Lord.

1. What good news does Revelation 21:2b

bring us? _____

2.   What does Revelation 19:7 tell us to do? _____

_____

What is the reason according to verse 8? _____

_____

"Come, I will show you the *bride,* the wife of the Lamb" (Revelation 21:9). This is a picture of all glorified saints. They adore the Bridegroom, not themselves!

The Bride eyes not her garment But her dear Bridegroom's face;
I will not gaze at glory But on my King of grace.
Not at the crown He giveth But on His pierced hand:
The Lamb is all the glory of Immanuel's land.

Anne Ross Cousin

Permanent Dwelling Places

"In My Father's house are many *rooms*; if it were not so, I would have told you. I am going to prepare a place for you" (John 14:2). Another phrase for "rooms" (μοναι) would be permanent dwelling places. There is only one house in heaven, the Father's house. Everyone lives in this house. The picture is one of intimate fellowship with God and with everyone there (We will study this in greater detail in the next lesson). This is paradise regained, but infinitely greater than that in the Garden.

Is there someone here who is not a believer in the Lord Jesus as his personal Savior? God is not offering you a $500,000 home in some prestigious part of town. He is offering you a mansion in heaven where the streets are paved with gold. If you are not a believer you are saying, "I really  don't want to live in heaven some day." What is your problem? It won't be long and you'll say good-bye to Kansas (or whatever state you live in) and to this earth. *Where are you going to move?* I know where I'm going and so do others in this class. In the words of the old spiritual:

I've got a home in gloryland that outshines the sun,
I've got a home in gloryland that outshines the sun,
I've got a home in gloryland that outshines the sun —
    'Way beyond the blue.

The second stanza:
    I took Jesus as my Savior, you take Him, too —
    While He's calling you.

Their Condition

What we will have in heaven we did not take with us. Someone said, "There are no luggage racks on hearses." What we will have will be gifts from our Lord. Someone said, "Describe heaven to me so I'll want to go." And God does. "Be all that you can be," the U.S. Army says. They can't do it, but God can, and some day He will in heaven. What will we be? What will we have?

1. *Perfect joy! Pleasure! Comfort! Laughter!* Divide into five groups, one for each verse, and answer: What does God promise us in —

   Psalm 16:6b? _____

   Psalm 16:11b? _____

   Isaiah 35:10? _____

   Luke 6:21b? _____

   Luke 16:25b? _____

   These are dominant characteristics of heaven, and they overflow heaven right now. Heaven is all of the above. Satan and the demons who follow him cannot know heavenly experiences. They are "happy" only when men remain in unbelief. The holy angels, however, have joy every time a sinner repents (Luke 15:10).

   True or False: The joys of heaven seem to be a shared experience.

2. *Complete knowledge!* Here is an amazing wonder. "Now I know in part; then I shall *know fully*, even as I am *fully known*" (1 Corinthians 13:12b). Many commentators believe that St. Paul now knows fully, for example, both the mystery of his election and conversion. The saints in glory have a knowledge which

penetrates completely. We shall know God directly and completely. It appears that there will be no limits either to depth or degree of knowledge and understanding. The knowledge of God will take priority over all other subjects. Why do you think this is true? _____

_____

What other knowledge do you look forward to receiving? _____

_____

_____

3. *New bodies!* Are you ready to trade the old one in for a brand new one? Oh, the aches and pains! There is a tombstone in a cemetery near Milwaukee which says, "I told you I was sick!"

Joni Eareckson Tada puts it in words.

> I can hardly believe it. I, with shriveled, bent fingers, atrophied muscles, gnarled knees, and no feeling from the shoulders down, will one day have a new body, light, bright, and clothed in righteousness — powerful and dazzling.
>
> Can you image the hope this gives someone spinal cord-injured like me? Or someone who is cerebral palsied, brain-injured, or who has multiple sclerosis? Imagine the hope this gives someone who is manic depressive. No other religion, no other philosophy promises new bodies, hearts, and minds. Only in the Gospel of Christ do hurting people find such incredible hope.
>
> It's easy for me to "be joyful in hope," as it says in Romans 12:12, and that's exactly what I've been doing for the past twenty-odd years (*Heaven Your Real Home*, p. 53).

Hurray for all the saints who suffer physical pain on this planet! A new day is coming, and what a happy day it will be. St. Paul writes, "The Lord... will transform our *lowly* bodies so that they will be like *His glorious body*" (Philippians 3:21b). What were some of the characteristics of Jesus' glorified body after His resurrection? _____

_____

When Jesus took Peter, James, and John to the Mount of Transfiguration we read, "Just then there appeared before them Moses and Elijah, talking with Jesus" (Matthew 17:3). Where were Moses' and Elijah's bodies just prior to this? _____

All three bodies were "in glorious splendor" (Luke 9:30) as their bodies appear in heaven; however, their glorious appearance was subdued enough so that the eyes of the three disciples were not blinded. Moses' and Elijah's bodies maintained their identity. Peter, James, and John recognized them without being introduced. Which important chapter of the Bible deals most exclusively and exhaustively with the resurrection of the body? _____ Read 1 Corinthians 15:42-44.

What is the natural body? _____

What is the spiritual body? _____

What words are used to describe our new resurrected bodies?

4. *A new heart!* How desperately we need new hearts. God's plea to Israel and all men is this: "Rid yourselves of all the offenses you have committed, and get a *new heart* and a new spirit. Why will you die, O house of Israel" (Ezekiel 18:31)? Even after we repent and believe in the Lord as our Savior we still carry with us a spirit that delights in sin.

We agree with Joni Eareckson Tada:

That's why the best part of heaven will be a purified heart. I'm reminded of this every time I recite those beautiful words in the General Confession from *The Book of Common Prayer* that say,

Almighty and most merciful Father; we have erred and strayed from thy ways like lost sheep. We have followed too much the devices and desires of our own hearts. We have offended against thy holy laws. We have left undone those things which we ought to have done; and there is no health in us... miserable offenders.

I love those words. And I hate those words. I'm weary of constant confession. I despise sinning. It pains me to keep erring and straying, to do things that I shouldn't do, to always fall face-flat in the dirt, grieving that I miserably offend the God I love. My heart is soiled and stained, and that drives me to the Lord on my knees (at least, metaphorically). What's odd is, the closer I draw to Jesus, the more intense the heat of the battle.

Never do I feel more on the frontline of this battle than when I offer praise to God. Right in the middle of adoring Him in prayer or singing a praise hymn, my heart will start wandering off into some wicked thought. I have to grab my heart by the aorta and jerk it in line time and again! (*Heaven Your Real Home*, p. 40).

How does Romans 8:23 shed light on the above dilemma?

_____

_____

What effect will no more sin have on us in heaven? _____

_____

_____

5. *Christlike!* " "For those God foreknew He also predestined to be *conformed to the likeness* of His Son" (Romans 8:29). We will be like Jesus: holy, glorified, powerful, eternal, and spiritual. His body after the resurrection gives us a hint of what we will be like. Though the doors were locked, He appeared bodily in the room (John 20:19,26). The disciples thought they were seeing a ghost until He held out His nail-pierced hands and said, "Touch." Jesus ate after His resurrection even though He didn't

need to. We will be like that. We will be ageless and not experience the many limitations we are now so familiar with. We will not know pain, sorrow, sickness, or tears. In other verses we are told that we will shine like the stars forever and ever.

Concluding Thoughts

A man by the name of Aristeides wrote a letter around A.D. 125 to one of his friends in an attempt to explain the unbelievable success of Christianity. Here is one sentence from the letter: "If any righteous man among the Christians passes from this world, they rejoice and offer thanks to God, and they escort his body with songs and thanksgiving as if he were setting out from one place to another nearby."

There is a lot about heaven we cannot understand. "Now we see but a *poor reflection*; then we shall see face to face" (1 Corinthians 13:12). But what we do see from here is more than enough to cause us to rejoice. We confess with David, "In righteousness I will see Your face; when I awake, I *will be satisfied* with seeing Your likeness" (Psalm 17:15).

1. Write down the name of the state you live in: _____

    Would you like to live there for the next one thousand years?

    _____ Why? _____

2. Do you believe beyond a shadow of a doubt that you will be

    satisfied when you awake in heaven? _____

    Why? _____

3. True or False: Some days I am ready to go to heaven that very moment, and on other days I'd rather stick around for awhile.

    How come? _____

4. How do you suppose Joni Eareckson Tada would answer both

    parts of question 3? _____

5. Recently I received a nice card from a former member of my flock (twenty-seven years ago). She was kind in her thoughts. The cover of the card really caught my attention: "In my Father's House are many mansions. I hope yours is next to mine!" Do you suppose that in heaven you'll wish you lived closer to certain people (and tell why)? _____

6. True or False: The saints in heaven are presently thrilled over their citizenship, that they are the Bride of Christ, their permanent dwelling places in the Father's house, their joy, pleasure, comfort, laughter, knowledge, their new hearts and so on. They have no regrets over leaving earth for heaven.

7. How can the saints on earth presently be a little more like the saints in glory? _____
   _____
   _____

Closing Hymn

I'm but a stranger here, Heav'n is my home;
Earth is a desert drear, Heav'n is my home;
Danger and sorrow stand Round me on ev'ry hand;
Heav'n is my fatherland, Heav'n is my home.

Therefore I murmur not, Heav'n is my home;
What e'er my earthly lot, Heav'n is my home;
And I shall surely stand There at my Lord's right hand.
Heav'n is my fatherland, Heav'n is my home.

Closing Prayer

Lesson 4

THE MANY WONDERS OF HEAVEN

The Wonder of God's Family

How many times have we witnessed a scene like this at an airport? Loved ones whom we have not seen for a long, long time are greeted with tears and hugs and laughter. "How are you?" "You look so good." "I've missed you." I know. I have family scattered around the country. I don't get to see them often, and I miss them. There is something wonderful about family.

One of the most frequently asked questions directed to pastors is: "Will I know my loved ones in heaven?" The answer is, "Yes, and even better than you knew them on earth!" But there is more, so much more to the wonder of God's family in heaven and that is the lesson before us. Let's take a peek.

Opening Hymn

Sing the wondrous love of Jesus, Sing His mercy and His grace;
In the mansions bright and blessed, He'll prepare for us a place.
When we all get to heaven, What a day of rejoicing that will be!
When we all see Jesus, We'll sing and shout the victory!

While we walk the pilgrim pathway Clouds will over spread the sky;
But when traveling days are over Not a shadow, not a sigh.
When we all get to heaven, What a day of rejoicing that will be!
When we all see Jesus, We'll sing and shout the victory!

Opening Prayer

O God, in great love You sent Your only Son from heaven to earth that You might some day take us from earth to heaven. You know better than we what it is like to lose a son in death. Not only that, but in Your great love for us You nailed Him to a cross. You charged all our sins to Him. You punished and killed Him. Oh, how You must love us! Oh, how Jesus must love us! Please wrap your arms of forgiveness around each of us right now so that some day we may wrap our songs of praise around You. We know a little about family here on earth. Help us learn more about the wonder and splendor of our heavenly family, our forever family. We ask this as Your dear children in the dearest name of them all — Jesus! Hallelujah! Amen.

God

In anticipation of our arrival in heaven, whom do we want to see first of all? Eighteenth century hymn writer Fanny Crosby expressed so well what our answer will be:

> Through the gates of the city in a robe of spotless white,
> He will lead me where no tears shall ever fall;
> In the glad song of the ages I shall mingle with delight —
> But I long to see my Savior first of all.

You should know that Fanny Crosby was blind. When she died, the very first person she saw was Jesus Christ. It will be wonderful to meet our loved ones. It will be exciting to visit with Biblical saints and to see where we will live in our Father's house. Our greatest delight by far, however, will be to know and see God and His Son in undiminished and infinite splendor.

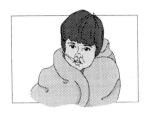

I hold before you your little sister in the faith — Patti. Six years old. Leukemia. A member of my flock at Gary, IN. As death came nearer, my visits to her in the hospital became frequent. One day we finished our devotions together. She sat on the edge of her bed, legs dangling down. Her face was puffed up. It was getting close now. And so I asked her, "Patti, what's going to happen to you?" With a big smile she answered, "Oh, I'm going to heaven." I said, "But, Patti, what's so special about that?" And with a twinkle in her eyes and with utter joy in her voice she replied, "I'm going to see Jesus!" Thank You, Jesus, for Patti! If a little six year old girl can know and confess such joy facing death, then you can, too. You're going to see Jesus, and that will change everything. Hallelujah!

1. What does Revelation 21:3 say about God's family (Dig deep; what does it really say)? _____

    _____

2. We long to be with Jesus. How does Jesus feel about us according to John 17:24? _____

    Why? _____

3. What do we learn about a person who says to a homeless, hungry, and destitute beggar, "I would like you to be a special guest in my home, and I will provide for you."? _____

    What do we learn about the beggar if he accepts? _____

    _____

    What do we learn about the beggar if he declines? _____

    _____

    Apply the above three questions to spiritual reality. What are the conclusions? _____

_____

4. How do you respond to a friend who says, "I really have no interest whatever in going to heaven and seeing God."? _____

_____

5. Why do you want God to be number One in heaven? _____

_____

God alone makes heaven a place of indescribable splendor. There are many attractions in heaven, but one stands out over all the rest: "You guide me with Your counsel, and afterward You will take me into glory. *Whom have I in heaven but You?* And earth has nothing I desire besides You" (Psalm 73:24-25). What does the italicized sentence suggest? _____

_____

What does the last sentence suggest? _____

_____

Angels

 "Angel" comes from the Greek word *angelos* (ανγελοσ) and means messenger or representative. The word "angel" is used over 300 times in Scripture.

The family of God in heaven includes angels. Many people believe that when they get to heaven they will become angels. A New York cemetery has a tombstone epitaph which reads:

> Sacred to the memory of Mary Flynn,
> Who was so very pure within,
> She burst the outer shell of sin,
> And hatched herself a cherubim.

That is amazing and not Biblical! There are even a few hymns in some Christian hymn books which suggest that saints become angels in heaven. Angels, of course, are special creatures who carry out God's will on earth and in heaven. They do not have bodies but do occasionally take on human form. (The author has written an extensive Bible study entitled, *The Story of Angels*. See page 108 for more details). Divide into groups. Each group look up one or more of the following verses and answer: What do we learn about angels in

Daniel 7:10b? _____

Luke 15:10? _____

Hebrews 1:14? _____

Hebrews 12:22? _____

1 Timothy 5:21? _____

Matthew 18:10b? _____

Revelation 5:11-12a? _____

Revelation 7:11-12? _____

Revelation is the ANGEL BOOK in the New Testament. Angels are everywhere. Heaven is their home. We will share it with them.

True or False: Chances are we will be mesmerized by the worship of angels in heaven and will not be able to take our eyes off them. Defend your answer.

Animals

There is a story (author unknown) entitled *The Rainbow Bridge*. The first two paragraphs tell how, when an animal dies, it goes to Rainbow Bridge where they are all happy and content except for one small thing: each of them misses someone very special, someone who was left behind. The third paragraph reads —

They all run and play together, but the day comes when one suddenly stops and looks into the distance. His bright eyes are intent; his eager body begins to quiver. Suddenly, he breaks from the group, flying over the green grass, faster and faster. You have been spotted, and when you and your special friend finally meet, you cling together in joyous reunion, never to be parted again.

The happy kisses rain upon your face; your hands again caress the beloved head, and you look once more into those trusting eyes, so long gone from your life, but never absent from your heart. Then you cross the Rainbow Bridge together...

We recently put our little Bichon Frise named Katie to sleep. It was so difficult to do this. We miss her. What a unique gift from God. She was "family." Some of you know what I'm saying because of a very special animal God has put in your life.

Will animals be in heaven? They are mentioned frequently from Genesis to Revelation. Nowhere does the Bible say that animals have an immortal soul or that they fit into the main purpose of heaven nor does it specifically say they won't be there. Some Bible commentators observe that since God placed animals on earth at the creation as a gift to man, it is not unreasonable to assume that He will do the same for heaven. God's promise is that heaven will be perfect with or without them. Of course, many of us are hoping it will be with them.

People

1. ***The numbers!*** Revelation 7:4, "Then I heard the number of those who were sealed: *144,000* from all the tribes of Israel." Most conservative theologians agree that the 144,000 represents all of God's people.

> The 144,000 symbolize the Church of Jesus Christ of all ages. In 4:4 and elsewhere the twenty-four elders represent the twelve patriarchs of the Old Testament and the twelve apostles of the New Testament, 12 + 12 = 24. Now our formula changes to 12 X 12 = 144. The number 12 is representative of God's people, the Church, especially when it is multiplied; and there is further multiplication: 10 X 10 X 10 = 1,000. Ten symbolizes completeness, particularly on earth. One thousand, the product of 10 X 10 X 10, means magnitude or vastness. When 1,000 is multiplied by 144, we see a beautiful symbolism of God's people, spiritual Israel, spanning the centuries (*Unlocking the Mystery of Revelation*, pp. 46-47, by James H. Knotek).

Which words in Revelation 7:9 emphasize the enormous number of saints? _____

_____

These people comprise the sum total of the fruit of the Gospel and of all mission work. Not everyone will be there. In fact, most people will not be there. Our Lord is emphatic on this point: "Enter through the narrow gate. For *wide* is the gate and broad is the road that leads to destruction, and *many* enter through it" (Matthew 7:13). Yet, heaven will be full, full of people who were made holy by a saving and personal faith in their Savior.

2. ***Identity and recognition!*** Read Genesis 25:7-8. The last six words are used frequently in the Old Testament and implied that the individual maintained his identity. David's child died, and David said, "But now that he is dead, why should I fast? Can I bring him back again. *I will go to him*, but he will not return to me" (2 Samuel 12:23). David knew that both would retain their identities. At Jesus' Transfiguration Peter, James, and John instantly recognized Moses and Elijah (Matthew 17:3). They needed no introduction. We, too, will recognize Moses and Elijah and all the inhabitants of the holy city.

3. ***Happy reunion!*** Fanny J. Crosby writes —

When our eyes behold the city with its many mansions bright
And its river, calm and restful, flowing free,
When the friends that death hath parted shall in bliss again unite,
What a gath'ring and a greeting there will be!

When my sister, Donna Mae, was three years old and I four years old, we contracted whooping cough and pneumonia. She died. The only recollection I have of her is her funeral. I can still clearly see her casket in our home (that was a custom then), watching my mother place a little gold cross in her hands, and then I cried as the hearse took the casket to the church for the funeral service (I had to remain at home). I can tell that my parents, faithful followers of the Savior at New Ulm, MN, missed her very much.

Now for an interesting observation on the happy reunions that take place in heaven. There may be times when it even begins on the deathbed of a Christian. Billy Graham, for example, tells how his maternal grandmother died. He says that she sat up in bed and said, "I see Jesus... I see Ben (her husband who had died some years earlier), and I see the angels" (*Angels, Angels, Angels,* p. 152).

I confess that I have doubted the validity of claims like this until my father's death. He was in his hospital room at 7:00 a.m. and was unconscious. Just before he died my sister says that he spoke these words loudly and clearly, "Mother" (that's what he called my mom), "Donna Mae!" She said that it was obvious he had seen Donna Mae just before he died.

While there is no Scriptural basis for it, perhaps the Lord gives this privilege to some of His children just before they leave earth. This I know for sure: we will see our loved ones who died in the Lord again in heaven. What a happy day that is going to be. We will never say good-bye or goodnight again. Oh, how we thank the Lord. Thank You, Jesus, for this great reunion that has already begun and which we will join real soon!

Read 1 Thessalonians 4:13-17. What are we told not to do?

_____

Why? _____

What are we to do according to verse 18? _____

Let's do that right now here in class for a few moments!

How are unbelievers described in verse 13? _____

What do they do when loved ones die? _____

Will we believers in heaven know if any of our unbelieving loved ones are missing? No, they will not be remembered (Psalm 69:28 and Psalm 109:13). This is the eternal tragedy of unbelief (Mark 16:16). How should we talk to our unbelieving loved ones about this? _____

4. *Unity, closeness, and equality!* God's children on earth frequently have trouble with these qualities. "At that time the disciples came to Jesus and asked, 'Who is the *greatest* in the kingdom of heaven?'" (Matthew 18:1). In Matthew 20:20-28 a mother asked Jesus to give her two sons positions of honor in His kingdom. That caused some real problems with the disciples. Jesus taught that while there are degrees of glory in heaven, selfish ambition, rank or position would be absent. The many rooms in our Father's house suggests closeness. St. Paul reminds us in Galatians 3:28: _____

5. *Marriage temporary!* Read Matthew 22:30. In what way will we be like the angels in heaven? _____

Why will there be no marriage in heaven? One reason would be that there is no need for procreation there. Another might be that in Eden Adam needed a helper and Eve a provider. That situation is different in heaven. St. Paul is emphatic that marriage is binding in life, but it is cancelled at death (Romans 7:2).

What do we say to a married person who says, "I can't think of being happy in heaven without being married to my spouse."?

_____

True or False: Scripture seems to present our earthly families as a microcosm of our one heavenly family.

True or False: Our relationship in heaven first with Jesus and then with the family of God will be infinitely better than any pleasure or fellowship we experienced on earth.

True or False: Former husbands and wives will still know, appreciate, and enjoy each other in heaven.

6. *Conversation, laughter, joy!* Years ago an elderly couple, missionaries, returned from a lifetime of service on foreign soil. On the same boat the President of the United States and his party were also arriving from a foreign tour. Great crowds of people greeted the President, but there was no one there to welcome the missionary and his wife. Afterward, in the hotel room, the old

missionary cried and said, "We spent our lives on a foreign mission field, and no one was there to greet us when we came home." The thoughtful wife said, "But darling, we aren't home yet." Indeed, many Christians have had to endure many trials in this world. When you experience burdens and trials, remember, you are not home yet. There is about to be a massive change! And you will love it!

A number of verses allude to our eating in heaven. With eating comes conversation and fellowship. Will there be humor? Chances are, but not at anyone's expense. Laughter? Yes. Jesus contrasted the two worlds when He said, "Blessed are you who weep now, for you will *laugh*" (Luke 6:21b). Even now our *joy* is in the Lord (Romans 5:11).

Concluding Thoughts

1. What might we talk and laugh about in heaven? _____

    _____

2. What makes heaven precious to us (give this careful thought)?

    _____

    _____

3. Of the many wonders of heaven, God's family is unique. What aspect of God's family will amaze you the most? _____
    Why? _____

4. The wonders of heaven are many and amazing. Why is it, then, that you are not always excited about going there? _____

    _____

    Why is it that whenever a brother or sister in Christ gets close to going Home to enjoy everything we have learned so far, we immediately form a prayer chain (one as big as possible), and we try to talk God out of taking our Christian friend to heaven?

    _____

5. Many of us are privileged to belong to happy, caring, and functional families here on earth. How will our forever family in the Father's house be more wonderful by far (think of the details

of this Lesson): _____

_____

_____

Closing Hymn

Let us then be true and faithful, Trusting, serving every day;
Just one glimpse of Him in glory Will the toils of life repay.
When we all get to heaven, What a day of rejoicing that will be!
When we all see Jesus, We'll sing and shout the victory!

Onward to the prize before us! Soon His beauty we'll behold;
Soon the pearly gates will open — We shall tread the streets of gold.
When we all get to heaven, What a day of rejoicing that will be!
When we all see Jesus, We'll sing and shout the victory!

Closing Prayer

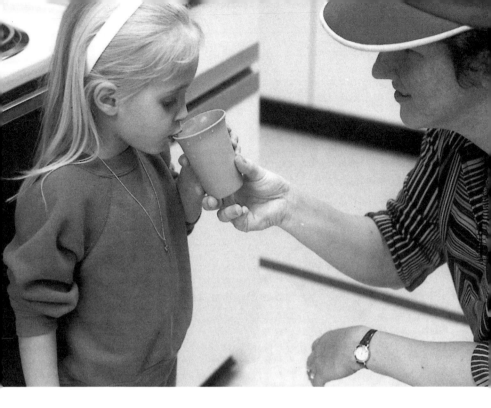

Lesson 5

THE MANY WONDERS OF HEAVEN

The Wonder of Reward

Jesus says: "I tell you the truth, anyone who gives you a cup of water in My name because you belong to Christ will certainly not lose his *reward*" (Mark 9:41). Heaven will have many surprises for us, among them is that of rewards for service rendered in Jesus' name. Notice how He begins His statement: "truth." Any assistance, no matter how small, if given out of love to the Savior, will certainly be rewarded.

Jesus leaves unsaid what the reward will consist of. The reward may come here or in heaven. We occasionally hear believers say, "I don't care if I am rewarded for anything in heaven — I just want to make it there." Such well intended thoughts demonstrate a serious lack of understanding of what the Lord taught (1) about living our lives to His glory here on earth and (2) about how He will surely reward it in heaven.

Opening Hymn

Take my life and let it be Consecrated, Lord, to Thee;
Take my hands and let them move At the impulse of Thy love,
At the impulse of Thy love.

Take my feet and let them be Swift and beautiful for Thee;
Take my voice and let me sing Always, only for my King,
Always, only for my King.

Opening Prayer

Dear Lord Jesus, no obstacle was too great, no burden too heavy, no sacrifice too costly when You came to earth to serve and save us. We, however, have often been hesitant to serve You by serving others. Time and again we have stood idle. Repeatedly we have been reluctant to be Your hands and feet to a hurting world. O Lord, please forgive us for our thoughtlessness and selfishness. Give us Your spirit of sacrificial love and service so that in the judgment we who were first may not end up being last. Teach us how important works of love are to You. Teach us how You will wonderfully reward them in heaven. In Your name. Amen.

Introductory Thoughts

There once was a very rich man who "wanted to take it with him" when he died. He prayed and prayed until finally the Lord gave in, but on one condition — he could only bring one suitcase of his wealth. The rich man began to worry, "What kind of currency should I bring — the dollar, the pound, the yen, the mark?" He finally decided that the best thing to do was to turn all of it into gold bullion. The day came when God called him home. St. Peter greeted him, but told him he couldn't bring his suitcase in with him. "I have an agreement with God that I can take it with me," the man explained. "That's unusual," St. Peter said. "This has never happened before. Mind if I take a look?" The man opened the suitcase to reveal the shining gold bullion. "*Pavement!*" the amazed St. Peter exclaimed, "Why in the world would you bring *pavement?*"

God's children are not to be overly concerned about laying up for themselves treasures on earth. That's what the Jewish religious leaders did in Christ's day. Our Lord saw this and said: "Do not store up for yourselves *treasures on earth*, where moth and rust destroy, and where thieves break in and steal. But *store up for yourselves treasures in heaven*, where moth and rust do not destroy, and where thieves do not break in and steal. For *where your treasure is, there your heart will be* also" (Matthew 6:19-21).

It is true that we Christians normally conclude that we will take nothing in this world into heaven. In reality that is not correct. Our Lord teaches us to invest heavily in people and the Word. Both are eternal, but so is something else. Many times the Lord brings up a third element like this: "But love your enemies, do good to them, and lend to them without expecting to get anything back. Then *your reward will be great*, and you will be sons of the Most High, because he is kind to the ungrateful and wicked" (Luke 6:35). St. Paul is even more direct when he reminds the Philippians, "Not that I am looking for a gift, but *I am looking* for *what may be credited to your account*" (4:17).

The following two quotes are helpful.

> Rewards are offered by God to a believer on the basis of faithful service rendered after salvation... Often in theological thinking salvation and rewards are confused. However, these two terms must be carefully distinguished. Salvation is a free gift... whereas rewards are earned by works... The doctrine of rewards is inseparably connected with God's grace. A soul is saved on the basis of divine grace; yet there is no room for the building up of merit on the part of the believer. Yet God recognizes an obligation on His part to reward His saved ones for their service to Him. Nothing can be done to merit salvation, but what the believer has achieved for God's glory, God recognizes with rewards at the judgment seat of Christ (*The New Unger's Bible Dictionary*, p. 1080, by Merrill F. Unger).

Scripture teaches that the good works of Christians receive a reward, yea, a very great reward. The false connotations which have been connected with this word "reward" must not deter us from using it. We shall unresistantly teach, both publicly and privately, that God rewards the good works of Christians here in time and, particularly, in eternity. But this reward... must be regarded strictly as a reward of grace... He who hands God a bill for his good works places himself outside the Kingdom of Grace. This double truth, namely, that God rewards good works, but that no man may demand this reward as his right, as earned by him, is brought out clearly in Matthew 19:27–20:16 (*Christian Dogmatics*, Vol. III, p. 10, by Francis Pieper).

Some times the Lord drives home His admonition to not store up treasures down here but up there. Back in 1997 there were some very destructive floods in parts of North Dakota and Minnesota. Thousands of people lost everything they had. I remember seeing a poignant picture — mostly a pile of rubble made up of soaked carpet, ruined appliances, insulation, lumber, etc., that had been pulled from what was left of a house behind it. In large letters someone had made this sign and planted it in front of the rubble: "Store your treasures in HEAVEN." That is God's advice for His children everyday, even when the sun is shining brightly. Let's take that advice right now and act on it. We'll never regret it. That's one of the many wonders of heaven!

Service Here — Rewards There

1. When a wealthy man entered heaven, St. Peter gave him a bicycle to ride over the golden streets. Pedaling along, he saw his butler go by in a Cadillac and his gardener driving a $200,000 Lamborghini Diablo. Very upset, he went to St. Peter and asked why his butler and gardener had more luxurious transportation than he did. St. Peter explained, "The kind of transportation you are assigned in heaven depends on how many and how good your good works really were as a Christian on earth." Two days later the man returned to St. Peter, and he was laughing. "What's so

funny?" St. Peter asked. "Yesterday I saw my pastor going by on a pair of roller skates."

True or False: This story tells me how my pastor will get around in heaven.

True or False: This story suggests that there is a direct connection between good works here and rewards there.

2. What does the Bible say? "For we must all appear before the judgment seat of Christ, that each one may *receive what is due him for the things done* while in the body, whether good or bad" (2 Corinthians 5:10). This is a public judgment before all men and angels in contrast to the judgment which takes place at the moment of death. All of us will stand for judgment before the all-knowing and all-righteous Judge. This verse does not speak of "work righteousness," but rather those deeds and actions which flow either from saving faith in Christ or from unbelief.

3. Briefly, what is taught about works and rewards in the following verses (be precise)?

    Matthew 5:11-12 _____

    Matthew 19:29 _____

    Matthew 23:11-12 _____

    Matthew 25:19-21 _____

    Mark 10:43-44 _____

    Luke 14:13-14 _____

    Ephesians 6:8 _____

4. Mention several general truths from Matthew 10:41-42: _____

    _____

    _____

5. What do you think the Lord is trying to get across in all of these Scripture verses? _____

    _____

6. True or False: The bottom line is that there are earthly rewards and heavenly rewards, and it's okay to go after them. Defend your answer.

Various Rewards

1. A few years ago a man named Ron Hoover went through a Bible study course I had written, *I Have Good News For You*, where his soul was converted. When we came to the lesson on Christian stewardship his pocketbook was "converted." He became a tither. Then something interesting happened. Ron's business took off and money poured into his pockets, so much so, that one day he asked if he could stop by for a visit. When he arrived he told his story of soul and pocketbook conversion. However, because of the huge increase in income, Ron said that his tithe offerings were really getting big. "Is there some way," he asked, "that I can cut these large offerings down a bit?" I said, "Ron, I can think of only one way." "Good," he said, "what is it?" I said, "Ron, in a few minutes you and I will kneel down in front of these two chairs, and I will ask the Lord to reduce your income so that your offerings are not so high." He was in shock. In a few seconds he said, "No, I think I like it the way it is." You should know that Ron continued to tithe because of his child-like faith in the Lord. A few years later, at age 43, he became exceedingly wealthy — he joined the angels and saints in glory.

    How is it with you? Do your offerings express your sincere love to the Lord in view of Calvary? Tithing is not commanded in the New Testament, but sacrificial and cheerful giving is. Too many Christians want to give the Lord small gifts of love now; however, they will receive less from Him in heaven. Do you think Ron Hoover is happy now that he gave sacrificially? Yes, indeed! And you can be, too! You may want to read Malachi 3:8-10 and Luke 6:38. Both passages stress the wonder of reward.

2. Rewards hang in the balance for everything you do and which

you don't do. These rewards will vary according to the work. "The man who plants and the man who waters have one purpose, and *each will be rewarded according to his own labor*" (1 Corinthians 3:8). Notice that these are solemn promises by almighty God.

True or False: One would be wise in putting off dwelling on the above truths until about a year before he dies. Defend your answer.

3. There will be at least two kinds of reward in heaven. One kind of reward will be that of responsibility. How is that brought out in the following passages?

Matthew 24:45-47 _____

_____

Luke 19:16-19,26 _____

_____

Are these verses having any kind of effect upon you? _____

_____

4. Beside the reward of responsibility in heaven (we will study this in greater detail in the next lesson), there will be rewards of adornment. What two very special works and rewards are

mentioned in Daniel 12:3? _____

_____

5. Not only will there be different kinds of reward in heaven, but there is also the possibility that a believer can be very misguided and end up with precious little in heaven. Read 1 Corinthians 3:11-15. Paul depicts for us two kinds of believers who are built

upon _____ The first group of believers are those who build with gold, silver, and costly stones which are more valuable and abiding materials by far compared to the second group of believers who build with wood, hay, or straw which are not valuable and not abiding. The Corinthians are examples of people who seemed to use wood, hay, or straw, but Paul still calls them brothers in Christ. The works of believers will be tested by

_____ on the Last Day. If what a believer has

built is burned up, he will suffer loss, although he himself will be
_____ What does this say about our works and rewards?

_____

Give some examples of what determines if a person is in the first
group: _____

_____

Give some examples of what determines if a person is in the
second group: _____

_____

6. What does all of this do to the statement by a few believers, "I
don't care if I am rewarded for anything in heaven — I just want
to make it there."? _____

_____

True or False: The above means that there just might be some
slightly surprised saints in heaven.

What should all of this encourage us to do on a regular basis?

_____

Why? _____

Why do you suppose that many conservative, Gospel-minded
congregations seem to overlook the above in their teaching?

_____

Name one group of believers who will receive special recognition
in heaven (Revelation 6:9-11): _____

_____

7. Read Joni's statement on 1 Corinthians 3:10-15 and briefly
comment on those sentences that stand out for you.

I'm constructing with an eye toward eternity, and so can you.
Every day we have the opportunity to roll up our spiritual
sleeves and apply our spiritual energies toward building

something that lasts, in our lives and the lives of others. We are warned to be careful and choose as our building materials gold, silver, and costly stones; that is, service rendered out of a pure heart, a right motive, and an eye for God's glory. Or we can choose wood, hay, or straw; things done out of an impure motive and an eye to our own glory.

We will bring to the judgment seat of Christ all that we are and all that we've done. One look from the Lord will scrutinize the quality of what we've built, and selfish service will be consumed in a fiery flash. Although it's true that no child of God will be scolded, some will walk away scalded from the heat; their only reward will be their eternal salvation.

This is sobering. I can't help but see myself coming away a little singed on the edges. Don't get me wrong, I believe I will bask in God's approval for my service on earth, but pride and impure motives have probably sullied a lot of it. Burnt away will be those times I gave the gospel out of puffed-up pride. Up in flames will go any service I performed for "performance's sake." Reduced to charcoal will be manipulative behavior and lies-dressed-up-like-truth (*Heaven Your Real Home*, p. 59, by Joni Eareckson Tada).

Served By Jesus

Read Luke 12:35-37. Jesus uses the picture of a great Lord whose servants (disciples) are always ready to serve and wait for their master to return. "Return from *a wedding*" refers to the great celebration which took place when Jesus returned to heaven after working out the redemption of mankind. That marriage feast is now in progress in heaven and will continue forever. The

> **He makes His servants lords and serves them**

disciples on earth are serving Him and waiting for Him. On the Last Day Jesus will come back to earth in great glory to take His servants Home. Then, astoundingly, He does not make other servants serve them, but He serves them! He makes His servants lords, and He Himself becomes their Slave!

How do we know this is true? _____

"He (Jesus) will dress Himself to _____ (them), will have them recline at the table and will come and _____ on them."

It is wonderful to think of seeing Jesus, of worshiping Him, yet, as incredible as it seems, that joy will be taken to even greater heights as He serves us forever! Yet, this heavenly act should not surprise us too much. "You know the grace of our Lord Jesus Christ, that though He was *rich*, yet for your sakes He became *poor*, so that you *through His poverty* might become *rich*" (2 Corinthians 8:9).

How did the Lord of heaven and earth do this? Jesus "made Himself nothing, taking the very nature of a *servant*, being made in human likeness. And being found in appearance as a man, He *humbled* Himself and became *obedient to death* – even death on a cross" (Philippians 2:7-8). On the night before His death He washed His disciples' feet because He loved them.

Why do you suppose Jesus wants to serve you forever in heaven?

_____

Why do you want to daily and gladly serve the Lord with good works?

_____

Motivation

We live in a very sinful world. Our motivation for good works as Christians is in need of some heavenly guidance. What guidance is given in these verses?

Matthew 6:3-4 _____

Matthew 5:11-12 _____

Luke 14:12-14 _____

1 Corinthians 10:31 _____

Let's look at just one Old Testament believer. "Moses regarded disgrace *for the sake of Christ* as of *greater value* than the treasures of Egypt, because he was *looking ahead to his reward*" (Hebrews 11:26).

Let's not underestimate the treasures of Egypt; they were exceedingly great. When Moses compared all the treasures of Egypt to that of heaven, it was really no contest. On the other hand, we find the choice much more difficult. Why? _____

_____

The reproach that Moses suffered was a priceless honor as he looked at Jesus (remember that he had to see His Savior off in the future). What seems to happen to us when we are called on to suffer "disgrace for the sake of Christ"? _____

_____

Beside Moses' great love for the Messiah (remember that he even wrote about Him in Deuteronomy 18:15-19), he "was looking ahead to *his reward*." Moses kept his eyes on things not seen as did Abraham, David, Paul, and many other saints. Work at keeping your eyes on things not seen, on the rewards waiting for you in heaven. Eliza E. Hewitt wrote:

Let us then be true and faithful, Trusting, serving every day;
Just one glimpse of Him in glory Will the toils of life repay.
When we all get to heaven, What a day of rejoicing that will be!
When we all see Jesus, We'll sing and shout the victory!

Concluding Thoughts

1. Joni Eareckson Tada —

> When a Christian realizes his citizenship is in heaven, he begins acting as a responsible citizen of earth. He invests wisely in relationships because he knows they're eternal. His conversations, goals, and motives become pure and honest because he realizes these will have a bearing on everlasting reward. He gives generously of time, money, and talent because he's laying up treasures for eternity. He spreads the good news of Christ because he longs to fill heaven's ranks with his friends and neighbors. All this serves the pilgrim well not only in heaven, but on earth; for it serves everyone around him (*Heaven... Your Real Home*, p. 110).

2. Someone said, "Where we bank is even more important than what we bank." Many financial institutions in our country have folded and at great expense to all taxpayers. What two things in heaven could we lose? _____

3. Read Revelation 22:12. We will not be rewarded because of our good works, but we will be rewarded according to our good works. What is the difference? _____
    _____

    True or False: According to this verse both unbelievers and believers will be rewarded for their deeds by the Lord, the first group's deeds flowing out of unbelief and the second group's deeds flowing out of saving faith.

4. What advice does 2 John 8 have for us? _____
    How could that be done? _____

5. People say, "You can't take it with you!" Do you agree? Why?
    _____

6. Is heaven where your heart is? _____

7. True or False: In view of Bible truth, if you wish to be miserable, focus on this earth, and if you want to be joyful, focus on heaven. Defend your answer.

8. Joni Eareckson Tada —

    God gives us a twenty-four-hour slice of time in which to make the most of every opportunity, opportunities that will have eternal repercussions. The way we spend... the hours and moments counts. It counts far more than we realize (*Heaven... Your Real Home*, p. 204).

    How does Joni's first sentence impact on you? _____
    _____
    _____

How do Joni's second and third sentences impact on you?

_____

_____

Closing Hymn

Take my lips and let them be Filled with messages for Thee;
Take my silver and my gold, Not a mite would I with-hold,
Not a mite would I with-hold.

Take my love, my God, I pour At Thy feet its treasures store;
Take myself and I will be Ever, only, all for Thee,
Ever, only, all for Thee.

Closing Prayer

Lesson 6

THE MANY WONDERS OF HEAVEN

The Wonder of Activity

This is James Luca trying to sing from his hymnbook. He has just been told by his pastor that in heaven he will sing forever and ever. He'll never stop singing to God. Wow! That's heavy. Can you imagine any boredom that could be greater in his mind? He can't sing most of the tunes — can't pronounce half the words. And the lady behind him is singing loud and very much off key. Forever?

And when his Sunday School teacher later asks him, "James, aren't you happy that you're going to heaven?" what do you think his answer might be? Many of us have shared his thoughts. When I was his age I thought, "How boring. We'll just sit there and twiddle our thumbs!" If there is anything that frightens people about heaven, it has to be the fear of boredom. We're here to discover that it will be anything but boring with little to do.

Opening Hymn

For all the saints who from their labors rest,
All who by faith before the world confessed,
Your name, O Jesus, be forever blest. Alleluia! Alleluia!

The golden evening brightens in the west;
Soon, soon to faithful warriors comes their rest;
Sweet is the calm of paradise blest. Alleluia! Alleluia!

Opening Prayer

Dear Lord Jesus, You came from heaven to earth to work out our salvation. Among Your last words from the cross were these: "It is finished!" You have told us that You have gone back to the Father to prepare a place for us. You have sent the Holy Spirit to create saving faith in our hearts. We cannot praise You sufficiently for all that You have done. As we look forward to joining You in heaven we wonder, "What will we do there?" Make this Bible study a response to that question. Fill each of us with an even greater anticipation of the perfect joys that await us in the new heaven and new earth. In Your name we pray. Amen.

Will It Really Be Rest?

Of all the tombstone epitaphs dealing with rest in heaven, the following may say it best:

Here lies a poor woman who was always tired,
For she lived in a place where help was not hired.
Her last words on earth were, "Dear friends, I am going
Where washing ain't done, not sweeping, nor sewing;
And everything there is exact to my wishes,
For where they don't eat, there's no washing dishes.
I'll be where loud anthems forever are ringing;
But having no voice, I'll get rid of the singing.
Don't weep for me now, don't weep for me ever;
For I'm going to do nothing forever and ever."

Now, that doesn't sound like fun, does it? Will heaven be like these three definitions?

- Erick Jones, age 7, said, "It's a place where there's a lot of money laying around. You can just pick it up and buy things. I'm going to buy a basketball and play basketball with my great grandmother."

- Daniel Reagan, age 7, said, "It's like a blue sky with clouds and it's a really fun place because you can play on the clouds. You have to stay away from the edges though or else wow — you'll fall off!"

- David Drennan, age 5, said, "Heaven is sort of big and they sit around and play harps. I don't know how to play a harp, but I suppose I better start to learn how pretty soon."

Is heaven a Christian nirvana where we will do nothing but sit on the edge of a fleecy cloud, dangle our legs over the edge, and play a harp? What kind of rest will we have?

Hebrews 4:1 speaks of every one of God's people "entering his *rest*." Chapter 4 describes an eternal Sabbath rest in heaven which simply means that we will never be tired or unfulfilled. It will be a very unique rest.

Revelation 14:13 reads: "They *rest* from their labor." Many of the saints while on earth labored hard to maintain their faith and their faithfulness. The price was often high, but in heaven they rest from such weary labor. What an eternal relief! It will be the opposite for those eternally lost. "There is *no rest* day or night for those who worship the beast and his image" (verse 11). What an eternal burden! Beside sweet rest from earthly burdens, heaven will be filled with joyful, challenging, exhilarating activity.

Fellowship

1. There will be the activity of fellowship with God.

   Read John 17:24. What does Jesus want?

   _____

   We long to be with Jesus, but He longs

even more for us to be with Him. Why is this? _____

_____

He desires full, unhindered fellowship with us and we with Him.
What do you suppose this fellowship might consist of? _____

_____

Why is there no danger of this fellowship ever becoming boring?

_____

Read Revelation 21:1-3. There was a time when God had an
earthly dwelling place, the first Tabernacle and then the Temple.
Jerusalem became the holy city, but God rejected this nation
because it had rejected Him. No more Temple. Now Jerusalem is
above. John, in his vision, saw the new Jerusalem (which we will
study in detail in the next lesson). What is the Temple now called

in verse 3? _____

Why are the people in verse 8 not there? _____

How is the dwelling of God actively described in verse 3? _____

_____

_____

How is this the fulfillment of "Immanuel"? _____

_____

2.   I shall never forget a visit I made during my vicarage year from
     the seminary at a congregation in Hobart, IN. One of the
     members asked that I visit her grandfather who was up in years.
     He had no time for God or the church, but, the member added,
     "He very much misses our son who died when he was six years
     old." For two hours I tried to explain to the old gentleman God's
     love and his need for a Savior — to no avail. I finally asked if he
     missed his grandson. "Oh, yes, very much!" "Where is he now?"
     "He is in heaven." I said, "You're right, but I have bad news for
     you. You'll never enjoy him again. He was a believer in Jesus and
     is now in heaven, and you are an unbeliever and will go to hell."
     With that the old man began to cry and said, "I could never stand

that! Tell me more about Jesus!" I did. He came to faith that afternoon. Later he died. Now he enjoys his grandson and all the children of God.

What does 1 Thessalonians 4:18 tell us to do and why? _____

_____

_____

Do you think it was proper to tell the grandfather the things

mentioned above? _____ Why? _____

_____

Pass it on

Do you think you should ever be this blunt with some of your unbelieving friends? _____

Why? _____

_____

Have someone in the class who has done this share the situation.

3. We will have fellowship with everyone, and things that make fellowship difficult on earth will be gone. What are some of the

things here that hinder fellowship? _____

_____

We will experience relationships in heaven unlike any we have developed on earth. Added to the relationships of the saints with each other and with God, we will also relate to the angels. What a glorious fellowship awaits us!

Eating

Ah, now we have your attention.

"Are all here?" someone will shout. There will echo, "Yes, we are all here!"

Now, enjoy an unseen divine reality. Rev up your heart and picture yourself taking a seat at the Wedding Supper.

Open the eyes of your heart and marvel at the crystal-clear glory, the dazzle of light that just *is*. A holy city, the New Jerusalem sparkling like a prism. And a banquet hall resplendent with banners, color, stunning with jewels and light-and-joy-filled music. The celebration will kick off with a loud and resounding "Hallelujah! For our Lord God Almighty reigns. Let us rejoice and be glad and give him glory! For the wedding of the Lamb has come, and his bride has made herself ready" (Revelation 19:6-7).

As you pull up a chair to the banquet table, take a look at what's on the menu from Isaiah 25:6-8: "On this mountain the Lord Almighty will prepare a feast of rich food for all peoples, a banquet of aged wine — the best of meats and the finest of wines. On this mountain he will destroy the shroud that enfolds all peoples, the sheet that covers all nations; he will swallow up death forever. The Sovereign Lord will wipe away the tears from all faces; he will remove the disgrace of his people from all the earth. The Lord has spoken."

There's no mistaking. This is a real banquet. And a specific one too. They won't be serving bologna or Spam. It won't be USDA-approved meat; it will be "the best of meats." And the beverage selection will not be Kool-Aid or cheap wine, but "aged wine... the finest of wines." (*Heaven Your Real Home*, p. 150, by Joni Eareckson Tada).

Can you eat all you want in heaven and never get fat? Jesus eating breakfast with the disciples after His resurrection, the marriage supper of the Lamb, the Lord serving us, and other events seem to indicate that we will eat. The real focus of heaven will not be the food, but Jesus, the Bread of Life. What do you suppose will be the purpose of such eating? _____

Rejoicing

The Bible is emphatic when it says that one of the great wonders of heaven will be rejoicing. Even now Jesus is the source of our abiding joy and happiness. "You will *fill me with joy* in Your presence, with eternal pleasures at Your right hand" (Psalm 16:11). Your cup of joy will run over!

It's hard to wait when you're in love. I want to see Jesus and so do you! So — "Let us *rejoice* (in our hearts) and be *glad* (in every outward demonstration) and give Him glory! For the wedding of the Lamb has come, and His bride has made herself ready" (Revelation 19:7). The old marriage custom must be remembered. First the betrothal was made public by the two families. This made the two participants legally husband and wife; no priest was needed to officiate. An interval of time followed. Finally, the group led a festal procession to the bride's home where she had made herself ready. The groom then took his bride, along with his friends and relatives, to his own home where festivities continued for a week or longer. The wedding was concluded by the bride and groom entering the bridal chamber. The saints (the Bride of Christ) are to rejoice, for the wedding festivities in heaven have begun. They will never end!

Rejoice!

> Then, oh, what jubilation To see our Savior's face,
> His glorious exaltation Since winning us God's grace.
> Then kings will come to meet us And psalmists rich in song,
> Apostles, prophets greet us, A great and splendid throng.
>
> Johann Walter

Why do you think God paints the above picture for the saints (the Bride of Christ) still on earth? _____

_____

Worship and Praise

1. Remember the boy in the picture at the beginning of this Lesson? Well, Mark Twin had an even poorer concept of singing in heaven. He wrote:

   > It goes on, all day long and every day... the singing of hymns alone, nay, it is one hymn alone. The words are always the same, in number they are only about a dozen, there is no rhyme, there is no poetry: "Hosannah, hosannah, hosannah, Lord God of Sabbaoth, Rah! Rah! Siss! Boom! Ah" (*Letters From The Earth*, p. 17)!

If he thinks the singing in heaven is boring, one wonders what he thinks of the singing (the Bible calls it wailing) in hell.

2.   Read Isaiah 6:1-4. Here two groups of _____ bring forth antiphonal shouts. What do they shout? _____

What effect did the sound of their voices have? _____

_____

_____

Does it sound boring? _____ While there were other glimpses of heavenly worship given in the Old Testament, the most extensive insights will be found in the book of _____

3.   Recently we were privileged to listen to Johannes Brahms, *Ein Deutsches Requiem, Opus 45.* During the concert I thought to myself, "Unbelievers cannot offer this kind of music." Like Handel, Brahms lifts up the Lord's people still on earth. And, yet, as beautiful and stirring as this music is, it will pale in every respect when compared to what we will hear soon in heaven where no composer or conductor of music is needed.

Hallelujah!

4.   Read Revelation 14:2-3. What does verse 2 suggest? _____

_____

What points are stressed in verse 3? _____

_____

_____

Why is it that unbelievers cannot learn the new song? _____

_____

5.   Revelation 4 is the "Throne Chapter." Scan verses 8-11. Note the spontaneity and enthusiasm of the worshipers. They are moved to lay even their crowns before the Lord. The crowns are symbols of victorious royalty which were wholly derived from Him who sits

upon the throne.

6. Revelation 5 is the "Lamb Chapter." Scan verses 9-14. The song is "new." The old song of the old covenant spoke of the Lamb to come. The new song says that the Lamb has been slain, His blood has cleansed God's people, and redemption is complete.

Why do they sing in a loud voice (v. 12)? _____

_____

True or False: Chances are they are singing words already written for them.

What is the major motif of their great praise? _____

_____

"Amen" is a powerful word meaning true or truly, a seal of verity.

> In all of the world's literature there are not many passages which even begin to approach the three grand doxologies of Rev. 5 in the full scope and forceful impact of their theme. It remained for George Frederick Handel to rise successfully to the challenge of setting the choruses in Rev. 5:12,13 and the "Amen" of Rev. 5:14 to the tremendous climax of instrumental and vocal music which brings his majestic and magnificent oratorio *Messiah* to an overwhelming close. No one who has ever been thrilled by an understanding performance of that world's masterpiece, involuntarily rise to his feet with the final "Amen," can ever forget the experience (*Revelation*, p. 91-92, by Luther Poellot).

7. As a group read aloud Revelation 19:1-10.

What picture is painted by select words in verse 1, end of verse 4, and verse 6? _____

_____

This entire episode depicts the love which the Groom (Jesus) has for the Bride (the Church). It is appropriately described in extravagant picture language. What did the angel assure John of in:

9a? _____

9b? _____

John is so overwhelmed by the revelation that he _____

_____ What is he told to do? _____

_____

8. We can identify with John's difficulty. I know that on any number
    of occasions, when singing special hymns of praise to the Savior,
    whether in a large gathering or small one, I find that I cannot
    sing. I am so moved by this corporate praise of Jesus who saved
    me that I can only stand there quietly and praise Him with warm
    tears from my eyes and gratitude deep from my heart. On those

occasions I usually look down, not wanting
anyone to see what I am experiencing within.
If we can be so deeply affected here on earth,
who can imagine what it will be like when we
join all the redeemed with Moses, Abraham,
Isaac, David, Matthew, Luke, Paul, our loved
ones and the myriad of angels, and with
trumpets and harps we present an outpouring
of joyful praise to the Lamb upon the
Throne?

When with the ransomed in glory His face I at last shall see,
'Twill be my joy through the ages To sing of His love for me.
How marvelous! how wonderful! And my song shall ever be:
How marvelous! how wonderful! Is my Savior's love for me!

Charles H. Gabriel

Serving

1. While halos in heaven are not mentioned in the Bible, serving is.
    I shared with my Bible class what I read in one book while writing
    this study. I mentioned that this author was sure that whatever
    our occupation was on earth we would do in heaven forever, only
    better. One sister in the faith whose name was Mona worked at a
    check out counter in a grocery store for the last twenty-five years.
    "You mean," she said with exasperation, "I'll have to do that
    forever?" I assured her, "No!" Let's see how we will serve.

2. Read Revelation 1:1. Here John is called a _____ of

   _____ Who is John to bring this revelation to?

   _____

   Revelation 5:10 clearly states: "You have made them to be a
   kingdom and priests to *serve* our God." Everything points to our
   serving role.

3. What does Revelation 7:15-17 tell us about our service? _____

   _____

   How do you know from these verses that the annoyances we

   normally associate with work will not be present? _____

   _____

4. No weakness or weariness will hinder us, and it will be our highest
   delight. We are reminded of our serving again in Revelation 19:5
   where we are called "servants" (δουλοσ). Again, "And His *servants*
   will *serve* Him" (Revelation 22:3b).

5. True or False: Our servant role for the Master begins the moment
   we become His children and will continue forever and ever.

6. What differences would you see between our service here and

   there? _____

   _____

7. What do you suppose our service will consist of there? _____

   _____

Reigning

1. Every believer on earth has been given certain spiritual gifts which
   are to be used to further the Lord's Kingdom. Just as we serve
   Him here and there, so there are spheres of responsibility here
   and there; included in this is the concept of reigning or ruling.
   For example, in Matthew 25:23 the master said to the responsible
   servant, "Well done, good and faithful servant! You have been
   faithful in a few things; I will *put you in charge of many things.* Come

and share your master's happiness!" There is a strong hint of new responsibility and authority in heaven. In some way our rule in heaven will be proportionate to our faithfulness to the Lord here. **It should be a sobering truth to us that our opportunities for responsibility in heaven are directly related to how faithful we**

have been on earth. Why? _____

_____

What immediate effect should this have on the use of your

spiritual gifts? _____

What can be done to increase the efficient use of *your* spiritual

gifts to the Lord's glory? _____

_____

Why is it so important that this answer be zealously pursued?

_____

_____

2. How do these Scriptures continue to drive home the above?

    2 Timothy 2:12a _____

    Revelation 3:21 _____

Concluding Thoughts

1. "And they will *reign* (as kings) *for ever and ever*" (Revelation 22:5b).

    In this Kingdom where God is King, where the Lamb is King, we shall be kings with them, a Kingdom unlike any that ever existed on the old earth... a Kingdom made up entirely of kings with a "King of kings" (*Revelation*, p. 655, R. C. Lenski).

    What do you like about the above? _____

    _____

    What mystifies you about the above? _____

    What does Revelation 22:6 tell you? _____

    _____

2. What has happened to even the tiniest thought of boredom in your new heavenly home? _____

    _____

3. In view of this Lesson, if you were an unbeliever, what would you want a Christian friend to tell you and when? _____

    _____

    _____

4. Write down the first names of two people who need spiritual help and try to do what you wrote above: _____

5. St. Paul tells us: "*You are the body of Christ,* and each one of you is a part of it. Are all apostles? Are all prophets? Are all teachers? Do all work miracles. Do all have gifts of healing? Do all speak in tongues? Do all interpret? But *eagerly desire the greater gifts*" (1 Corinthians 12:27,29-31). The word "gifts" is plural. God has given you many gifts. Stress the more important ones. Write down two spiritual gifts you would like to develop and how you will do it

    (Use class discussion on this): _____

    _____

    _____

6. When are you ready to go home? Why? _____

    _____

    _____

7. In this Lesson we looked at our activities in heaven: **fellowship, eating, rejoicing, worship and praise, serving, and reigning.** Do you think there is anything special you should tell your Lord today and every day (Think carefully about this and then do it)?

    _____

    _____

Closing Hymn

But then there breaks a yet more glorious day:
The saints triumphant rise in bright array;
The King of glory passes on His way. Alleluia! Alleluia!

From earth's wide bounds, from ocean's farthest coast,
Through gates of pearl streams in the countless host,
Singing to Father, Son, and Holy Ghost: Alleluia! Alleluia!

Closing Prayer

Lesson 7

THE MANY WONDERS OF HEAVEN

The Wonder of the City

Just a glance at this picture tells people immediately that it is Washington, D.C. Cities always seem to rise and dominate the land. Mention Washington D.C., and you think of the United States; Paris is France; London is England; Rome is Italy; Moscow is Russia; and Jerusalem is Israel.

Jerusalem. This, by far, is the most important city on earth for all time! 4,000 years of Old Testament history led up to it. God picked it. God lived there in a special way with His people. The cradle and the cross were nearby. Most of the people said "no" to Jesus. God finally left the city and destroyed the Temple.

God has now built a new Jerusalem, a city of unparalleled beauty where He lives with all His children. The city. What is it like? What are the sights, sounds, and smells of this eternal city? Let's try to see.

Opening Hymn

Crown Him with many crowns, The Lamb upon His throne:
Hark! how the heavenly anthem drowns All music but its own!
Awake, my soul, and sing Of Him who died for thee;
And hail Him as thy matchless King Through all eternity.

Crown Him the Lord of life: Who triumphed o'er the grave,
Who rose victorious to the strife For those He came to save;
His glories now we sing, Who died and rose on high,
Who died eternal life to bring, And lives that death may die.

Opening Prayer

Dear heavenly Father, in great compassion You called Your chosen people from Egypt and led them to the Promised Land. Jerusalem would have no military or economic advantage, but, Father, in Jerusalem You revealed salvation through Your Son. Please help Your pilgrims of this generation. We look for a new city, Jerusalem above. Father, help us see this City now by faith. Holy Spirit, enlighten our weak minds as we search the holy Scriptures that, learning more about Jerusalem the golden, we may yearn for the day when we say farewell to everything here and join You there. In the name of Jesus, our only Savior and Redeemer. Amen.

The Best Is Yet To Come

A clergy friend of mine pastors a congregation in Williston, ND. He told me about a Christian woman in his parish who was on her deathbed. In making plans for her funeral she told him, "When I am in my coffin I want you to place a fork in my right hand so that everyone can see it." Then she explained. "Whenever I served a nice meal and we had finished, before bringing out the desert I always said, 'Keep your fork. The best is yet to come.' When my unbelieving friends ask what the fork in my hand is for, I want you to tell them that for me the best is yet to come! And, then," she said, "explain to them how they can get to heaven, too, through Jesus." The pastor kept his promise, and many people were deeply moved. So much so that the next lady who prepared for her funeral requested that the pastor place a fork in her hand. You can understand why there is a run on forks in Williston. The best IS yet to come!

How would you describe America to someone who has never been here? If you lived in the northeast, you might describe the metropolis, New York City. If you lived in Kansas, you might describe the endless and rolling wheat fields. Someone from the west would speak of the blue Pacific Ocean. It would be difficult to describe this country to someone who has never been here and traveled here. The country is too vast and different to be adequately described from just one spot. The same is true of the new Jerusalem. It is mammoth in size and beyond description in beauty. And further, we have never been there. Some saints while on earth were given a view of the Holy City and came away breathless.

Read 2 Corinthians 12:2-4. Who was the man? _____

What did he see? _____

What is the "third heaven"? _____

Paul also called the "third heaven" _____

What effect do you think this had on his life? _____

_____

Jerusalem, my happy home, When shall I come to thee?
When shall my sorrows have an end? Thy joys when shall I see?

Jerusalem, my happy home, Would God I were in thee!
Would God my woes were at an end, Thy joys that I might see!

Anonymous

Prophesied

1. Read Isaiah 65:17-19. "Create" from *bara*, in the sense of calling into existence.

    What are we told to do (v. 18a)? _____

For how long? _____

The new Jerusalem will be a _____ and the people who

live there will be a _____ Are you ready for this? _____

What will the Lord do? _____

2. Read Hebrews 11:9-10. Abraham made his home in the _____

_____ but he was really a _____ in a

_____ I, too, am a _____ and

I live in a _____ Abraham did not spend

much time looking at where he lived, but in looking _____

to a _____ which was built by _____

What was Abraham looking forward to according to Hebrews

11:16? _____

What does this verse tell us about God? _____

_____

Cities on earth built by man don't last long — they fall apart. The
foundations of the city built by God suggest permanency — it will
stand forever. Abraham's thoughts always looked ahead to the
new Jerusalem. We, too, should spend less time looking at where
we live now and more time where we're going to live forever. How
can we be more like Abraham in this respect?

_____

_____

Read Hebrews 12:22-23. Another name for Jerusalem is Mount
Zion. Isaac Watts reminds us of this in his beautiful, "Come, We
That Love the Lord":

Come, we that love the Lord, And let our joys be known;
Join in a song with sweet accord, Join in a song with sweet accord
And thus surround the throne, And thus surround the throne.
We're marching to Zion, Beautiful, beautiful Zion;
We're marching upward to Zion, The beautiful city of God.

What three things is our eternal home called in verse 22? _____

_____

Verse 23 reminds us that the city is God's city. We believers are

called the _____ Our names are _____ A

permanent record has been made of our names.

Revelation 21 — 22:6 Describes The City

- **21:1** The old earth and sky had "fled from His presence, and there was no place for them" (A repeat of 20:11). 2 Peter 3:13 reminds us, "But in keeping with His promise we are *looking forward* to a *new heaven* and a *new earth*, the home of righteousness."

  There will be two basic differences between the old and the new. What is

  it spiritually? _____

  What is it physically? _____

  Why no more sea? It will not be needed.

- **21:2** What thoughts is God presenting to us when the Holy City is described as the Bride of Christ beautifully dressed for her

  husband which is Christ? _____

  _____

- **21:3-4** An unnamed voice speaks.

  The heaven of God and the new heaven and new earth created for men shall be joined, shall be the Holy City, New Jerusalem, God's Tabernacle with men, God tabernacling with them, they His people, He with them, their God. The final consummation of all God's plans in the creation of the world has been reached... No more dead bodies of saints in the graves on the old earth, no more souls of saints in the Jerusalem above, no more souls on the old earth in mortal bodies... In this vision the holiness of God's union and communion with us is stressed" (*Revelation*, pp. 619-620, by R. C. Lenski).

What is suggested by the words, "He will *live with them*"?

_____

The bliss of heaven is described in verse 4 in earthly, negative

terms. What are they? _____

In the last lesson we learned that we will labor in heaven. In view of the above verses what are some occupations here on earth

that will definitely not be needed there? _____

_____

● **21:5** John did not write these words on his own initiative. Like the other holy writers he wrote what the Holy Spirit moved him to write. We are not dealing with speculation or pie-in-the-sky. We must trust these words implicitly! Why? Who, specifically, is

making these promises? _____

● **21:6-8** "It is done." So that John can see it. Then Christ, if you will, signs His name to it. He is God's *revelation* from A to Z! He is the First and the Last *historically*! He is the Beginning and the End *redemptively*, from inception to consummation! John sees it all. So shall we! And it will be heaven!

Who are the thirsty? _____

_____

_____

ALLELUIA

What is the "drink"? _____

_____

Why is there no cost? _____

What will we inherit? _____

How does Luke 15:31b describe it? _____

The "cowardly" is a reference to those who gave up on the fight of faith. They will take their place in the fiery lake. Do you

know someone who is a spiritual backslider? _____

What can you do to bring that person back to the Lord's flock?

_____

The "vile, the murderers, the sexually immoral, those who practice magic arts" is a general reference to the heathen and to those who have activity with the great whore (Revelation 17:5-6). Idolaters would include those involved in emperor worship which was prevalent in Asia Minor at the time Revelation was written.

● **21:9-14** "The bride" and "the wife" refer to the moment of the nuptials when the Church on earth is united with and becomes the Church in heaven.

Washington, D.C., has so many sites to see that one has difficulty viewing them all. The new City is so glorious that John must view it from the vantage point of a great and high mountain.

Read verse 11 again. The glory of God, including all of His divine attributes, fills the Holy City. The "brilliance" is God Himself, more specifically, the Lamb, Jesus Christ. The City is clear, bright, and beautiful. The "great high wall" is not for protection, but is a symbolism of inclusion.

The 12 gates had written on them the 12 _____

The 12 foundations had on them the names of the 12 _____

The 12 tribes plus the 12 apostles represent _____

_____

● **21:15-21**

John continues to incorporate the multiples of twelve. The city's length, breadth and height are twelve thousand stadia each; the wall is one hundred forty-four cubits (12x12); and there are twelve jewels for its twelve foundations... The Lord is not giving statistics but, rather, symbols... The entire city is a perfect cube, just as the Holy of Holies in Solomon's temple was a cube that measured 20 cubits long by 20 cubits wide by 20 cubits high (1 Kings 6:20).

Imagine! Heavenly Jerusalem will be a giant Holy of Holies in which God's people will reside, for Jesus Christ has opened the veil so that you and I may enter and be welcomed by God Himself...

Not all twelve stones listed can be identified with certainty. The description is intended to dazzle the imagination and to carry the mind beyond its comprehension...

How can John convey the elegance and grandeur of this city in human words? He cannot. Our human vocabulary is too limited. No language on earth is capable of describing what John saw" (*Unlocking the Mystery of Revelation*, p. 137, by James A. Knotek).

If, out of simple human curiosity, we put the dimensions of the city into miles, it is a cube approximately 1,500 miles long, wide, and high; it would contain 2.25 million square miles. Here on earth 5,000 people can easily live in one square mile. On that basis 100 billion people could live there. When you look at verses 15-21, what is the first thought that comes to your mind? _____

_____

● **21:22-27** Of what does the temple consist? _____

How large an area does it occupy? _____

Where does the light for this city come from? _____

_____

"The nations" are all the glorified saints. "Kings" indicates that rulers of all kinds had crowned Jesus as their Savior and King while on earth, and they are in heaven.

There will be no segregation

by ethnic group or any kind of group. One story tells of a group of newly arrived Baptists being given a tour of the City. Each time they passed this one room the guide told them to be very quiet. Finally one of them asked why they were told to be so quiet when passing this one room. "Because," the guide said, "all the Lutherans are in there. They think they are the only ones up here, and we don't want to disappoint them!" Please note: religious denominations will be a thing of the past!

The wonder of the City continues. In Biblical times the city gates were shut at night for protection. The gates of this city are always open. This symbolizes perfect security, protection, and peace. In contrast the gates of hell are always _____

"The glory and honor of the nations will be brought into it" means that everything that nations and rulers did for the Lamb while on earth will be recognized and rewarded in heaven. Only those who put their faith and trust in Jesus will enter this great City. How is the place of the wicked described (v. 8)? _____

_____

- **22:1-5** What do we find in the Garden (Genesis 2:10)? _____

In the city of God, the Church on earth (Psalm 46:4)? _____

In the Holy City, heaven (22:1)? _____

In the latter verse, "river" is a collective noun, a river with a number of streams. It symbolizes life which comes from the Throne. This river of life branches out to all parts of the City. There is a beautiful park throughout the City. Better, there are many streets divided by little parks which are formed by the river and streams and trees. This is similar to how some of our modern cities are beautified.

The word "fruit" can be translated "crop." The thought is of no sickness, no hunger. The healing or health comes from the leaves of the tree of life or, again, from God. All of these terms, "river," "water of life," "great street," "tree of life," and "twelve crops" are comprehensive or collective and symbolize the perfection of heaven.

Life and perfection are found wherever you go in the City! Paradise lost is now Paradise regained and more! The opening chapters of Genesis tell of man in his innocence, then sin and fading joy. The closing chapters of Revelation tell of a new Paradise with unfading joy. God will again walk and talk with His people. What a wonder!

At last the march shall end, the wearied ones shall rest;
The pilgrims find their home at last, Jerusalem the blest.
Rejoice, rejoice, give thanks and sing!

Edward H. Plumtre

Concluding Thoughts

1. How can you tell deep inside that you're not home yet? _____

   _____

   _____

2. St. Paul said, "If I had my choice, instead of being an apostle, instead of being an evangelist, instead of being a preacher *I would prefer* to leave my body here on earth and be at home with the Lord in heaven" (2 Corinthians 5:8). Where would you rather be today? Bumper stickers say, "I'd rather be golfing." "I'd rather be dancing." Make your bumper sticker right now. Finish the following sentence truthfully.

   ┌──────────────────────────────────────┐
   │ **I'd rather be** _____   │
   └──────────────────────────────────────┘

3. In what ways is the city you live in (or near) different from the

   Holy City? _____

   _____

4. A national newspaper conducted a poll of some of the richest people in the country. The poll indicated that they would pay:

   $407,000 for great intellect
   $487,000 for true love, and

$640,000 for a place in heaven.

What conclusion does this lead you to? _____

_____

5. A few years ago an assistant pastor of a large church in Detroit phoned and thanked me for *The Many Wonders of Heaven* which their Bible class just finished. He then asked, "We would like to know what your sequel will be?" I thought for a moment and then said, "An eight lesson course titled, 'The Many Horrors of Hell.'" I could hear him tell the senior pastor this. There was a brief silence, and then I heard the senior pastor say, "It won't sell." Do you think he was right? _____ Why? _____

_____

6. List the names of three people you believe will be in heaven and tell why: _____

_____

List the names of three people you fear will be in hell and tell why: _____

_____

7. Of what does Revelation 22:6 assure us? _____

8. What does Jesus promise in Revelation 22:20a? _____

What should be our daily prayer (22:20b)? _____

9. "And so we will be with the Lord forever. Therefore *encourage each other* with these words" (1 Thessalonians 4:17-18). How can we go about doing this? _____

_____

_____

Closing Hymn

Crown Him the Lord of heaven: One with the Father known,

One with the Spirit through Him given From yonder glorious throne.
To Thee be endless praise, For Thou for us hast died;
Be Thou, O Lord, through endless days Adored and magnified.

Crown Him the Lord of years: The potentate of time,
Creator of the rolling spheres, Ineffably sublime.
All hail, Redeemer, hail! For Thou hast died for me;
Thy praise and glory shall not fail Throughout eternity.

Closing Prayer

THE MANY WONDERS OF HEAVEN

The Wonder of Anticipation

Columbine High School in Littleton, CO, is about three miles from our home. At ll:21 a.m. on April 20, 1999, two high school boys murdered twelve fellow students, one teacher, and then killed themselves.

John Tomlin was 16 years old, was active in mission work, and had a close relationship with Christ. A number of students committed themselves to the Lord at his funeral.

Rachel Scott, 17, was a committed believer who planned to go into missionary work in Africa. Her prom date shared how her faith had impacted on him and those around her in the school. More than 15 students committed their lives to Christ at the funeral.

Cassie Bernall was 17. Cassie was totally anti-Christian two years before. She was involved in witchcraft and very suicidal. Her parents forcibly brought her into a youth pastor's office. When she walked out his reaction was, "Wow, she is a lost cause..." Through the prayers of the youth group, parents, and youth pastor, Cassie, about six months later, went back to the youth pastor and said, "You'll never guess what I did today. I gave my life to Christ..."

From that point forward Cassie was a loving evangelist at school and with her friends. The funeral showed some video tape of her sharing her testimony which was very powerful. It appears that because of her faith she was singled out by the killers. One of the gunman asked her if she believed in God, to which she replied, "Yes, I believe in God (Some say she actually said "Jesus"). The funeral was a celebration of Christ's work in her and through her. At Cassie's funeral over seventy-five kids made first time commitments to Christ. Cassie's mother, Misty, writes:

One day a week or so before Cassie's death we were sitting at the kitchen table, talking, and got onto the subject of death. I don't remember how. She said, "Mom, I'm not afraid to die, because I'll be in heaven." I told her I couldn't imagine her dying — that I couldn't bear the thought of living without her. She replied, "But Mom, you'd know I was in a better place. Wouldn't you be happy for me?"

Through anecdotes we've heard from her friends, and through notes and letters we've come across since her death — we have begun to realize the depth of her innermost thoughts. In one of these notes, a scrap of paper marked "1998," she writes:

When God doesn't want me to do something, I definitely know it. When he wants me to do something, even if it means going outside my comfort zone, I know that too. I feel pushed in the direction I need to go... I try to stand up for my faith at school... It can be discouraging, but it can also be rewarding... I will die for my God. I will die for my faith. It's the least I can do for Christ dying for me (*She Said Yes*, p. 122, by Misty Bernall).

There are many wonders IN heaven, but there is also one that precedes it — the wonder of ANTICIPATION. Because of what awaits you in heaven, your life should never be the same. That is the exciting lesson in front of us.

Opening Hymn

(Stand)

All hail the power of Jesus' name! Let angels prostrate fall;
Bring forth the royal diadem And crown Him Lord of all.
Bring forth the royal diadem And crown Him Lord of all.

Sinners, whose love can ne'er forget The wormwood and the gall,
Go, spread your trophies at His feet And crown Him Lord of all.
Go, spread your trophies at His feet And crown Him Lord of all.

Opening Prayer

Dear Lord Jesus, we love You! We worship You! We praise You! You alone are the Son of God. You alone suffered and died to make us God's sons and daughters. Lord, take away all if's, perhaps' and maybe's. May our faith in You be "yea" and "amen." May we refuse to risk gambling our souls salvation by turning to anyone or anything but You! A thousand thanks for this Bible study and for all Your countless promises to us. Empower and enlighten us continually that we may be watchful and ready like the five wise virgins You once talked about. Dear Jesus, hear our cry for help to deal with the tears and trials of life. Be our strength when we are weak. Pick us up when we fall down. Precious Jesus, give us Your compassion for the lost. Help us invite them to our house of worship where they may hear the saving Gospel. Move each of us to tell our unbelieving friends what You have done for us and for them on Calvary. Remind us daily that we are not Home. Give us a longing to be with You and to join all the saints and angels in giving You perfect praise and service forever. We do not know when we will die. If we die before Your second coming, we want to awake in Your presence and we know we shall! Lord, all the signs about us indicate the end of the world is near. Come soon! Take Your pilgrims Home! In Your name, dear Lord. Amen.

Be Watchful

One of the saddest funerals I ever conducted was this one. There was a couple who received Biblical instruction and then joined our church. He weighed about a hundred pounds and she weighed about 250 pounds. Remember the weight. They seemed to believe in the Lord. With time, however, they stopped reading their Bibles, stopped attending church, and gave up their Christian faith. We were in the process of starting church discipline when, suddenly, he died. Since they were still on the church rolls, I was obligated to bury him. I want to tell you something — it's a very difficult thing to conduct a funeral at church when the deceased was not a Christian.

At the end of the service they moved his casket down the aisle while she followed right behind. Just as they passed the last pew she, in her uncontrollable grief, leaped up on the casket with all 250 pounds, screaming and crying. I thought, "Oh, no, she's going to break the casket and the whole mess will be on the floor." I have never witnessed such a spectacle in my life. The people who saw it were absolutely stunned. I want to tell you something: It pays to be alive and watchful in Jesus every day so that you are ready when He comes in the hour of death or the Day of Judgment. Listen up! Be wise! Learn from the Lord Jesus.

1. Read Matthew 25:1-13. It is difficult to imagine it, but five of the virgins took no oil for their lamps. Little wonder that they are called _____

2. Who is the "bridegroom"? _____

3. What does 5a tell us? _____

4. Who do the five foolish virgins represent? _____

5. What is the event in verse 6 called? _____

6. True or False: Verse 9 suggests that on the Last Day every believer will have sufficient saving faith for himself, but it cannot be

shared with anyone else.

7. Describe the "foolish virgins" in the world today: _____

_____

8. Describe the "wise virgins" in the world today: _____

_____

9. What is Jesus' advice at the end of the parable? _____

_____

> The Bridegroom soon will call us, "Come to the wedding feast."
> May slumber not befall us Nor watchfulness decrease.
> But may our lamps be burning With oil enough and more
> That, with our Lord returning, We find an open door.
> Johann Walter

10. There is a wonder to our anticipating what lies just ahead for us in heaven. Write down keys words from the following verses that should encourage us in our daily anticipation of heaven.

Philippians 3:20 _____

Psalm 90:12 _____

Micah 7:7 _____

1 Corinthians 1:7 _____

Living Properly In The Last Days

The entire New Testament period is in reality the end or the Last Days. Living properly in these days is not easy. The devil, the world, and our own sinful flesh are at work on a daily basis to tempt and to discourage us. Many times we fight a losing battle. What do these Scriptures tell us?

2 Timothy 3:1-5 _____

Matthew 26:41 _____

1 Peter 5:8 _____

What encouragement do the following Scriptures give us?

Romans 8:37 _____

2 Timothy 3:16-17 _____

Hebrews 10:24-25 _____

A businessman had this sign on his desk:

> **In 20 years what will you
> wish you had done today?
> Do it now!**

That's a great question for every believer who seriously desires to go
to heaven. St. Paul wrote, "*One* thing I *do*" (Philippians 3:13), not,
"Thirty things I dabble in." It makes a very big difference what you are
doing, what you are focusing on every day — ask the five foolish and
five wise virgins. Do you want to be ready and waiting when Jesus
comes either in the hour of death or the Last Day? If you do, then
whatever it takes, do it and — do it now.

Do Not Lose Heart

1. It is very easy for all of us to get discouraged, but we can turn that
    discouragement into encouragement like the following:

    > Suffering makes us want to go there. Broken homes and
    > broken hearts crush our illusions that earth can keep its
    > promises, that it can really satisfy. Only the hope of heaven
    > can truly move our passions off this world — which God
    > knows could never fulfill us anyway — and place them where
    > they will find their glorious fulfillment...
    >
    > Some people have to break their necks in order to get
    > their hearts on heavenly glories above, and I happen to be
    > one of them. It was only after the permanency of my paralysis
    > sank in, that heaven interested me...
    >
    > My hope of running through earthly meadows and
    > splashing my feet in a stream will never come true — but it
    > will in the new heavens and new earth. My dream of hugging
    > a loved one and actually *feeling* his or her embrace will never

come true — but it will when we stand together before Jesus" (*Heaven... Your Real Home*, p. 182, by Joni Eareckson Tada).

2. List a few things which discourage you and cause you to lose heart? _____

3. What precise encouragement do the following passages give you? 2 Corinthians 4:16-17 _____

   _____

   Psalm 73:25-26 _____

   _____

   Romans 8:18 _____

   _____

4. What points of encouragement do you find in 2 Corinthians 5:1-9? _____

   _____

   _____

St. Paul writes, "We ourselves, who have the firstfruits of the Spirit, *groan inwardly* as we *wait eagerly* for our adoption as sons, the redemption of our bodies" (Romans 8:23). How is it to our benefit that we do not become too comfortable in this world?

_____

5. Jean Vandiver was a member of my last congregation. She was in her 70's and was suffering much from cancer. Only hours before she died, we finished a study on Psalm 23 and prayed together. Jean loved the Lord so much. Whoever lives next to her in heaven — wow! What a neighbor she will be. Her face showed that she was in considerable pain. I said to her, "Jean, let me ask you a question. Are you sure that you still want to believe in Jesus Christ as your Savior and die

with Him tonight?" There was a slight pause, and then, very quickly, this face which was racked with pain was filled, side to side, with the most beautiful smile you've ever seen in your life. She looked at me. Her eyes were alive with joy and in the warmest and sweetest voice I've ever heard she said, "Yes. Oh, yes." Then she faded off and a few hours later died. That is the wonder of anticipation as the saints suffer and do not lose heart.

We expect a bright tomorrow, All will be well;
Faith can sing through days of sorrow, All will be well.
On our Father's love relying, Jesus every need supplying
In our living, in our dying, All will be well.

Mary Peters

Sharing The Saving Gospel

I need to tell you one more thing about Jean. A few months earlier we made plans for her funeral. When we finished, Jean looked me in the eye and said, "There is one more thing. At my funeral service I want you to preach a strong sermon on Jesus, and when it is over, I want you to have an altar call, because some of my friends are not believers."

Now I have been in the ministry a long time, but I've never been asked to have an altar call at a funeral. I said, "Jean, you've got it." She earnestly wanted her friends and family in heaven. After the sermon we had the altar call. Seventeen people, including her son, Jim, confessed their sins and Jesus Christ as their Savior.

I hold before you your sister Jean as encouragement. As you anticipate your place in the Father's house with all the privileges that will be yours, is it not vital that you think about those people about you who have no such hope?

1. Until the Lord takes us Home He has work for us to do here. What do the following Scriptures tell us about this work?

    Matthew 9:37-38 _____

    Matthew 28:19-20 _____

    Acts 1:8 _____

    James 5:20 _____

Luke 15:4 _____

2. Think, for a moment, about how **easy** and **compelling** it is to tell the Good News of Jesus. Imagine that you were caught in a fire in a large building. You were trapped in this burning building, both your legs were broken, all your ribs are cracked (we're going to make this real bad), you can hardly breathe, you are pinned to the floor, fire is everywhere, you are ready to give up and die, and someone rescues you.

Could you imagine later on that one of your friends would say to you, "Hey, how did you get rescued?" And you reply, "I'm not going to tell you. It's a secret. Don't embarrass me by having to tell."

Would you do that? Then why be embarrassed to tell about your biggest Rescuer who saved you from the biggest fire, the fire of hell, who is your very, very best Friend and Savior, to whom you owe your life now and forever in heaven, Jesus Christ? Don't be embarrassed about Jesus. Be embarrassed if you don't talk about Him. You have a great story to tell, and you know some people who are "dying" to hear it! Tell it. Please? Here is a beautiful hymn that gives us a nudge:

Jesus! Oh, how could it be true, A mortal man ashamed of You?
Ashamed of You, whom angels praise,
Whose glories shine through endless days?

Till then — nor is my boasting vain —
Till then I boast a Savior slain; And oh, may this my glory be,
That Christ is not ashamed of me!
Gregg & Oliver

3. Personal evangelism falls into three simple categories. As a follower of Jesus you can do at least the first two.

   ● **Church Invitation** — The Christian invites people to come and worship with him. Over 70% of the folks who join a church were first invited by a member! That is amazing.

- **Witnessing** — The Christian simply tells others in his own words about what Jesus, his Savior, has done for him.

- **An Evangelist** — One who gives his witness of Jesus and then, by the power of the Holy Spirit, leads a person to confess his sin and embrace Jesus as Savior.

4. Read 1 Corinthians 9:19-20,22. Here I am encouraged to make

myself a _____ to _____ to _____ as many

_____ I will try to become _____ to

_____ that I might _____

This is how heaven's citizens act on their brief journey here on earth. Jesus reminds us, "Even *now* the reaper (soul winner) *draws his wages*, even *now he harvests the crop for eternal life*, so that the *sower* and the *reaper may be glad together*" (John 4:36).

> When I enter that beautiful City,
> And the saints all around me appear,
> I want to hear somebody tell me,
> "It was you who invited me here."

Longing For A Better Country

When I was five years old we lived in the little town of Nicollet, MN, population 600. Our church was that familiar white church building with a tall steeple. Before services each Sunday the church bell would ring. But it also rang throughout the year whenever a member died. It would toll slowly. I can still see my mother stopping whatever she was doing. She would count, and she would know who died; then she would say, "I'm so happy for..." (whoever it was that died). I could tell that she longed for heaven. Now she is eight-nine years old in a nursing home, and she *really* longs for heaven. Her daughter, Donna Mae, is there. Dad is there. She can't wait. I hope you're like that.

1. Read Hebrews 11:13-16.

What does verse 13 tell us about Abraham, Isaac, and Jacob?

_____

"Country of their own" in verse 14 might also be translated "fatherland."

> Unlike children of this world, these persons cannot settle down in some earthly place as their "fatherland" and feel fully satisfied and content there. They are born of God, they are children of God, this earth is not their home, and, although they are compelled to stay here, they constantly speak only as strangers and pilgrims speak and always show by this, show even unconsciously, that they are seeking for a fatherland in which they really belong *(Interpretation of Hebrews, James,* by R. C. Lenski, p. 397).

They were "longing" for heaven (verse 16). How do you suppose

they did this? _____

_____

2. How does a believer do what St. Paul instructs in Colossians 3:1-2?

_____

3. Read Psalm 73:25. What two great truths do you learn here?

_____

_____

4. How did St. Paul demonstrate his anticipation of heaven in

Philippians 3:13-14? _____

_____

5. True or False: It is sinful for a Christian to want to stay in this world rather than go to heaven. Defend your answer.

6. True or False: I'd rather have Jesus than anything this world could offer, and I'd rather have heaven than live on the most beautiful spot on earth.

The Assurance of Salvation

There is something very blessed about having the assurance of eternal life with God. Do you have it? Do you know for sure that if you died tonight you would immediately wake up in heaven? Some people believe that you cannot be that certain.

1. Why were the Scriptures written according to 1 John 5:13? ____

   _____

2. Paul tells us to do two things in Romans 10:9-10. What are they?

   _____

3. What does the Lord promise in John 3:36? _____

   _____

4. True or False: I have the solid assurance that because I believe in Jesus I have everlasting life. I have it **positively, absolutely!** God has **PROMISED** it! I **BELIEVE** it! That **SETTLES** it!

He Loves Me Always

Will God always put up with me and all my mistakes? A close pastor friend of mine called a few days ago. My son has cancer, and his wife has some precancerous tissue. We shared our concerns and our faith in the Lord. I then brought up the subject of God's tolerance with my repeated mistakes and sin in my life. During this conversation our little puppy, Lily, kept interrupting. She would bark. Then she found a bank statement and ate half of it. Then she had to go outside. I apologized for the dog's behavior. "She is embarrassing me," I said. Then brother Craig said, "You know, you and your puppy have a lot in common." He said, "Read Psalm 37:23, according to the *New Living Translation*." He quoted the verse for me:

The steps of the godly are directed by the Lord. *He delights in every detail of their lives.*

He said, "Your puppy can really do only two things: wag her tail and make a mess, and still you take delight in her. Sometimes that is about all we can do for the Lord: wag our tails and make a mess, and yet this verse says that God delights in every detail of our lives."

My friend, God delights in you, in every detail of your life. You are the "apple" of His eye. Don't let the devil or anyone else tell you differently. Let's treasure this truth now, and soon we'll enjoy it forever in heaven.

The End Is Near

"'Men of Galilee,' they said, 'why do you stand here looking into the sky? This same Jesus, who has been taken from you into heaven, *will come back* in the same way you have seen Him go into heaven'" (Acts 1:11). Jesus is coming. He will: **1. Come back visibly. 2. Come back bodily. 3. Come in glory**, and all the holy angels will accompany Him.

"The *end* of all things is *near*" (1 Peter 4:7). According to the Bible the world is a little over 6,000 years old. The Old Testament era is about 4,000 years. The Bible speaks of the time from Jesus' birth on as the last times, so, we have been living in the last times for 2,000 years. One of the marks of the first century Christians is that they believed in the imminent return of Jesus in the sky. They frequently greeted one another with the word, "Maranatha," which means, "The Lord is coming."

There is a brother in Christ who lived in the Midwest who had a beautiful habit. Every night after he prayed, he went to his bedroom window. He would look up into the sky and say, "Perhaps tonight, Lord?" In the morning, upon awaking, he would go to the same window and say, "Perhaps today, Lord?" Will you let God whet your appetite for the second return of Jesus like that? Perhaps tonight? Perhaps tomorrow? And let that impact on your thinking, on your emotions, on the things you decide to do and not to do, on everything. There is a awesome wonder in anticipating Jesus' second coming.

True or False: I believe that Jesus is coming in the sky very soon, even before I die (Tell why).

What Will Happen

Read Isaiah 35:10.

How do you plan to enter heaven? _____

How is your crown described? _____

With what will you be overcome? _____

What will leave you? _____

Finish then Thy new creation, Pure and spotless let us be;
Let us see Thy great salvation, Perfectly restored in Thee;
Changed from glory into glory, Till in heaven we take our place,
Till we cast our crowns before Thee, Lost in wonder, love, and praise!

Charles Wesley

After the closing hymn we ask that you have a prayer circle. Take a moment to jot down some thoughts which you would like to present

to the Lord in prayer: _____

_____

_____

Closing Hymn

(Stand)

Let ev'ry kindred, ev'ry tribe On this terrestrial ball
To Him all majesty ascribe And crown Him Lord of all.
To Him all majesty ascribe And crown Him Lord of all.

Oh, that with yonder sacred throng We at His feet may fall!
We'll join the everlasting song And crown Him Lord of all.
We'll join the everlasting song And crown Him Lord of all.

Closing Prayer Circle and Lord's Prayer

Singing of "Doxology" and "Abide With Me"

Praise God, from whom all blessings flow;
Praise Him, all creatures here below;
Praise Him above, ye heavenly host;
Praise Father, Son, and Holy Ghost.

Hold Thou Thy cross before my closing eyes;
Shine thru the gloom and point me to the skies;
Heaven's morning breaks and earth's vain shadows flee;
In life, in death, O Lord, abide with me.

He who testifies to these things says, "Yes, I am coming soon." Amen. Come, Lord Jesus. The grace of the Lord Jesus be with God's people. Amen (*Revelation 22:20-21*).

This Bible study written by Pastor Ginkel
120 pages, Leader's Guide available

 # The Story of Angels

Because of the intense interest in this topic, most study groups using this book double and even triple in size. Colorful and descriptive flyers permit you to imprint time and location of your class on your copy machine and may be used as handouts and bulletin inserts.

THEIR BEGINNING AND BEING
Their creation, their purpose, their home, their properties

SATAN AND THE FALLEN ANGELS
Their fall, their names, their power, their knowledge, on the attack, their defeat

ANGEL TITLES, NAMES, AND ACTIVITIES
Who they are, Michael, Gabriel, Cherubim, Seraphim

THE ANGEL OF THE LORD
Who He is and what He did in the Old Testament

GUARDING AND AVENGING ANGELS
Old and New Testament examples of what they did

WATCHING AND COMMUNICATING ANGELS
Old and New Testament examples of what they did

ANGELS AND JESUS
Before His birth, at His birth, lower than the angels, the temptation, in Gethsemane, at His resurrection and His ascension

EVIL ANGELS TODAY
Warning, the occult, witchcraft, Mormonism, New Age, Demon possession, near death experiences, Satan and Satanism, our victory

ANGELS AND BELIEVERS TODAY
Rejoicing, watching, guarding, and delivering

ON JUDGMENT DAY AND FOREVER
Introducing the Day, divide believers from unbelievers, execute judgment, evil angels, holy angels, our privilege and honor, closing thoughts

This Bible study written by Pastor Ginkel
Part 1 80 pages & Part 2 80 pages, Leader's Guide available

A Time To Laugh... Or Cry

What a delight it is to laugh and laugh hard. What a relief it is to cry and cry hard. *A Time To Laugh... or Cry* overviews the activity of man in the Old Testament – a time to cry because of man's stubbornness and sin and a time to laugh because of God's reaction to man's sin expressed in the Messiah. The thread of the Messiah is followed throughout. Each lesson begins with a contemporary introduction, hymn, prayer, explanation of text, probing and practical questions for discussion, plan of action, and daily Bible reading which correlates with the text being studied. A good dose of humor is interspersed throughout to attract attention and maintain interest.

Part 1   In the Beginning With Adam and Eve
In the Garden When Everything Went Wrong
At the Flood with Noah
When God Made A Promise to Abraham
When Abraham Faced the Supreme Test
When Jacob Received the Biggest Blessing
With Joseph the Slave, Prisoner, and Prime Minister
When God Called Moses to Lead Israel
When Israel Was Saved by the Blood of the Lamb
When God Gave the Law on Sinai

Part 2   When Israel Conquered Canaan
With Gideon, God's Man of Action
With Samson, Strong and Foolish
With David, the Soldier Boy and King
During the Building & Dedication of Solomon's Temple
At a Daring Contest of the Prophet Elijah
With Jonah, the Reluctant Evangelist
At What Isaiah Saw and Said
With Faithful Daniel and His Friends
At Malachi's Message of Despair and Hope

This Bible study written by Pastor Ginkel
112 pages, Leader's Guide available

I HAVE GOOD NEWS FOR YOU

*Over half a million copies sold world wide
in eleven languages and Braille*

A ten lesson course on basic New Testament Christianity using a catechetical approach and NIV text with brief conclusions. Each lesson has a closing prayer, hymn, daily Bible reading schedule, and challenging worksheet questions. Also available in large print for the visually impaired.

I HAVE GOOD NEWS FOR YOU about:
1. A God Who Cares For You
2. A Bible Which Guides and Frees You
3. A Savior Who Saves You
4. A Spirit Who Converts You
5. A Washing Which Cleanses You
6. A Meal Which Feeds You
7. A Devotional Life Which Blesses You
8. Keys Which Lock and Unlock
9. A Stewardship Which is Fully Committed
10. A Life Which Never Ends

Flyers describe the course (you put in where and when you meet). Ten 90 minute tapes, both video and audio, recorded live with Pastor Ginkel teaching. Can be used for make-up for those who miss a class or where a qualified teacher is not available.

This Bible study written by Pastor Ginkel
128 pages, Leader's Guide available

Getting Closer To God

Contains the basic truths of Scripture for juniors and adults. Passages are printed out with summary thoughts, suggested passages for memorization, closing hymn, prayer, Bible reading schedule for the week, and challenging worksheet questions.

Course fosters a clear, concise understanding of basic Christian doctrine in catechetical form with a strong emphasis on forgiveness of sins through Jesus alone in every lesson. A dose of humor is used throughout without showing disrespect for the teachings of Scripture.

GETTING CLOSER TO GOD

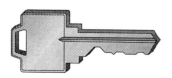 # Unlocking the Mystery of Revelation

Here is a Bible study which covers all of Revelation. Discussion questions at the end of each chapter. Excellent for Bible classes or individual study. Reflects a sound, Biblical method of interpretation allowing Scripture to interpret Scripture.

"I want to express my gratitude for *Unlocking the Mystery of Revelation.* I've been reading it and intend to use it as a source book for my fall Bible class. It's a **monumentum opus**! Congratulations on a beatiful job for Christ and His Church."

Dr. Oswald Waech

"Just a note to let you know how much I'm enjoy the study of Revelation by Pastor Knotek! Time flies so fast during the study that I can hardly wait for the next day!"
Dr. William Malcom, Jr.

"I want you to know how invaluable your book has been to our understanding of Revelation. I am one of the teaching leaders, and I personally was feeling somewhat overwhelmed last fall when I saw an ad for your book. Your material really helped things fall into place for me and for many in the class as well. Thank you!"

Marilyn Plechas

To order these Bible studies and other Christian materials and a brochure call our toll free number: 1-888-772-8878